The Art of
Living Alone
& Loving It

'But now I feel that solitude,
far from being the price,
is turning out to be the prize.'

ALIX KATES SHULMAN

The Art of Living Alone & Loving It

JANE MATHEWS

Your inspirational toolkit for
a whole and happy life

MURDOCH BOOKS
SYDNEY · LONDON

Published in 2018 by Murdoch Books, an imprint of Allen & Unwin

Murdoch Books
83 Alexander Street, Crows Nest, NSW 2065, Australia
Phone: +61 (0) 2 8425 0100
murdochbooks.com.au
info@murdochbooks.com.au

Murdoch Books UK
Ormond House, 26-27 Boswell Street, London WC1N 3JZ
Phone: +44 (0) 20 8785 5995
murdochbooks.co.uk
info@murdochbooks.co.uk

 A catalogue record for this
book is available from the
NATIONAL LIBRARY OF AUSTRALIA | National Library of Australia

A catalogue record for this book is available from the British Library.

ISBN 978 1 76052 361 9 Australia
ISBN 978 1 76063 458 2 UK

Cover design by Lisa White
Text design by Lisa White and Fleur Anson

Printed & Bound by MBM Print SCS Ltd. Glasgow.

10 9 8 7 6 5 4 3 2 1

To my kindred band of soloists:

this book is for you.

Contents

INTRODUCTION

I didn't choose to live alone. Few of us do. I fell into it post divorce – not with an elegant swan dive but with a graceless belly flop. Like a dodgy blind date, I can't say Living Alone and I hit it off straight away. But now I have learned not only to appreciate it, but even *prefer* it, and I can't see myself ever relinquishing my solo path. I don't see it as a compromise, a holding pattern or a bump on the road towards the sunny heights of coupledom. I am happy, but it took a while to get here.

There are three groups of soloists: never married or partnered; divorced; and widowed. A few have deliberately chosen a solo life, but the reality is that most of us have had our hand played for us. It doesn't matter whether it was choice or chance. Whatever got us to this point, we all want the same thing: not just to 'make the most of it', but to lead a textured, fulfilling life with joy in it. A life brimming with opportunities and potential, lived in Technicolor, not black and white.

With Dolby Surround Sound thrown in. A life in which I throw a pair of sixes more often than not, and can make my own memories. While researching this book, I spoke with many women who are living such lives. I came away deeply impressed and humbled. Their stories are quilted into the book. They swim in their independent waters like frolicsome otters, revelling in every twist and turn. I believe living alone *well* is a skill that isn't difficult, but requires some thought and effort. Like learning a language. In *The Art of Living Alone* I will share what has worked for me and for others.

Whether you view living alone as the ultimate compromise or the ultimate luxury, we all agree that it throws up daily challenges, such as cooking for one, organising a holiday, eating out alone, juggling finances, or trying not to succumb to the siren call of wine, Ugg boots and binge Netflix. And there are the less tangible tests, like nailing the octopus of loneliness to the wall, and holding your head high in a society where living alone is viewed (consciously or not) as synonymous with failure: the runner up prize.

If you are pretty happy with your lot and want a few tips to make living alone better, there are plenty in this book. If you are after more profound change, this book can also help. I believe that to be truly content living alone, it pays to scrutinise every aspect of your life, including your relationships, health, home, finances, interests and spirituality, and then take *action*. There's a chapter dedicated to each of these topics. Some of the suggestions will resonate, others won't, and that's fine. I'll provide the map and you choose the route.

Ten things I learned from writing this book:

1. Some of the strongest, most capable, most sociable, most loving people in the world live alone.

2. You have to like yourself. Nothing else will work until you nail this one.

3. Living alone is a skill that requires effort, but you will find strength you never knew you had.

4. Reframe the issue. Focus on living your life to the full. You just happen to live by yourself.

5. Being alone does not equate to being lonely.

6. You, and only you, are responsible for your happiness. It lies in your hands (the safest place for it).

7. Being alone gives you the time and space to unearth who you are and who you want to be.

8. Most people lie about what they eat alone.

9. The world belongs to those who do.

10. Tops with buttons up the back are Satan's triumph.

I feel a natural sense of camaraderie and empathy with other people who live by themselves. We are an amazing bunch, with so much to offer and so much going for us. I hope that you'll find some inspiration and useful ideas in the pages of this book. Think of it as a conversation with a friend.

You live alone,
therefore you are...

... lonely, sad, bitter, frustrated,
loveless, miserable, isolated, envious,
desperate, troubled, bored, boring,
solitary, depressed, scared, selfish,
vulnerable, excluded, overwhelmed, a
spinster, divorcee or widow, an old maid,
tragic, alienated, rejected, living a bleak life,
demoralised, ashamed, unloved, frightened,
strange, needy, inadequate, daunted,
financially disadvantaged, diminished,
belittled, desolate, odd, wretched,
unfortunate, pitiful, pathetic, regrettable,
friendless, companionless, defective,
forlorn, empty, separate, ashamed, a loser,
full of self-pity, invisible, unwanted,
unassisted, neglected, unmissed, forsaken,
abandoned, judged, lonesome, afraid,
compromised, a failure, bereft, insecure,
fearful, full of regret, anxious, self-absorbed
and one hundred per cent likely
to be a cat owner.

No! Not me. Not you.
Living alone offers us...

... freedom, pride, time, resilience, no judgement, independence, unexpected joys, flexibility, space to reflect, solitude, serenity, creativity, courage, self-understanding, opportunities to learn and explore, solo travel adventures, self-reliance, power, silence, the opportunity to discover who we are and want to be, freedom, relief from crowds, self-awareness, meaning, purpose, control, self-nurturing, freedom, authenticity, integrity, spontaneity, transformation, liberation, decadence, sense of mastery, self-esteem, space to sleep diagonally, self-sufficiency, thrills, autonomy, freedom, quiet, chance to be self-contained, peace, wholeness, strength, empowerment, space, tranquillity, opportunity, rectitude, potential, confidence, aplomb, self-possession, freedom, choices, a sanctuary, self-expression, chance to follow our instincts, peace and an untouched fridge.
Oh, and did I mention freedom?

Chapter 1

LIVING ALONE

Revised expectations ∗ *Society's assumptions*
∗ *We are a mighty army!* ∗ *Transformation*
∗ *Living with yourself, not by yourself*

I have succumbed to the siren call of my bed. Curled around my laptop, I am writing from my queen-sized oasis, dappled with wintery Sydney sun. The silence is occasionally interrupted by the squeaky call of a myna bird. I am still in my daggy walking pants from a yomp around the park with the dog at the crack of dawn. I am steeped in solitude. Unshowered. Unbreakfasted. It is midday. Sound familiar? The thing about living alone is that there is no one to criticise; no one to *critique*.

Much as I love the Land of Solo Living, it can be fraught with pitfalls, not least because it is always potentially trackpants o'clock. I reluctantly haul myself out of bed, shower and head to my desk downstairs. Not for the first time I am reminded that living alone requires discipline.

I share my house with too many cookbooks and a recalcitrant Airedale terrier, but no one with two legs. It took me a long time to appreciate living alone and there was much trial and error. I fell into solo living unexpectedly and, as the marital nest was hoiked away from under me, I was thrown back on my own resources, literally and figuratively. What started as tentative flapping has evolved, slowly and unexpectedly, into a confident soar. I now love living alone, and I am very good at it. Blimey. I never saw that coming.

You've got this

You are better prepared than you think. Think back to times in your life that have equipped you. Here are some of mine:

- A country childhood and a precocious, boy-loving older sister meant lots of time spent alone. *I've done this before!*
- Watching my mother abandon a career as a gifted fashion designer to fulfill the role of 1960s housewife and forever carry a tiny pebble of regret. *Do what you love!*
- Getting my first job and realising I was really good at it. *Channel that confidence.*
- Making a life in new countries, not knowing anyone. *I've proven my self-sufficiency.*
- Having children. *It's not just about me.*
- The feelings of immense sadness and rejection, like bullets in slow motion, following divorce and the death of my parents. I've been through worse before. *I am still loved.*
- First book being published. *I have a voice.*

I look back now and can see that when bad things happened to me I was building strength and capabilities with more power than I appreciated.

Strength + strength + strength × capabilities = power

You will have to draw on that power when living alone. Often it is not the big issues (loneliness, money, health, career, 'The Future', Christmas) that are the most challenging aspects, but the small relentless niggles – dripping taps, carrying lots of shopping bags, receiving bad news, taking the rubbish out, having no one to download to, cleaning up dog vomit when you get in from work, killing a cockroach, feeling unwell, moving heavy things, exasperating bureaucracy, running out of loo paper, or eating meatloaf three nights in a row – that threaten to overwhelm. Not being able to twist open the lid of a stupid jar can bring me to my knees. I am reduced to a puppet with my strings snipped. Sometimes I feel like a tiny figure under the towering surf of Hokusai's Great Wave.

You will get through that feeling, I promise. With a bit of effort, planning and being open to new experiences, over time it gets easier. You will find you are as capable as you need to be. More on this in the next chapter.

Revised expectations

My Dick and Jane reading books led me to believe I'd follow a certain life path, featuring a tall, lantern-jawed husband, a house with a picket

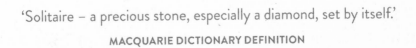

'Solitaire – a precious stone, especially a diamond, set by itself.'
MACQUARIE DICTIONARY DEFINITION

fence, shiny children who'd be content playing with wooden toys, and a perky dog with silky ears called Spot ('See Spot run!'). In the event the dog was the only part that manifested and, as I write, listening to the thrum of Rory snoring in a blissful farty sleep, I realise even that didn't go exactly according to plan.

I hadn't bargained on living alone, but now I wouldn't have it any other way. My expectations have been *revised*, not lowered, and in fact I set the bar much higher for myself than I ever would have as half of a couple or engulfed in a family situation. But of course it's not perfect: you have to be realistic and re-frame some assumptions.

How society sees us

There remains a stigma, for women more than men, about living alone in a society where couples and families are considered the norm. Small things signal your status, such as filling in a form with the options: never married/separated but not divorced/divorced/widowed/married (invisible sub-titles read *You missed the boat/Failure!/Failure!/Poor you/ Congratulations*). Where's the 'happily solo' option?

Sometimes the relentless conveyor belt of couples threatens to overwhelm, especially at restaurants and parties. The animals continue to plod up the gangplank into the ark two by two and you get the impression that 'Hold up, Mr. Noah! Party of one!' isn't in the script.

---
*

'Self-awareness is a supreme gift, a treasure as precious as life.'
IRVIN D. YALOM

I feel I am zigging while the rest of the world zags. We soloists are the outliers on the graph of society; a bit like being left-handed, but more so. It's a good analogy, because there are as many of us as there are lefties – about 10 per cent of the population.

Once you're attuned to it, you'll notice how readily and steadily the media embraces the lazy cliché of the Person Living Alone. Like Miss Lonelyhearts in Hitchcock's *Rear Window* or crazy DeDe in *Modern Family*, or the baddies in *Scooby Doo*, most of whom I am pretty sure lived alone in abandoned fairgrounds. Other clichés involve slit-pupilled cats who live for the day they can devour their mistress's corpse. Or lonely and bitter spinsters/divorcees/widows with freezers full of TV dinners, living life vicariously through reality TV and waiting for a man to rescue them. Like Miss Haversham, mourning a life that might have been. Or, lordy, lordy, poor Belle from Disney's animated *Beauty and the Beast,* who resorted to talking (or was it singing?) to the cutlery in the absence of any two-legged companions.

When I was a child, my older sister pointed out that because my third toe was bigger than my second I was a witch. No two ways about it. The proof was there for all to see. I ran crying to my mother, 'I'm a witch, I'm a witch – just look at my toes.' What a brilliant piece of manipulation on the part of my sister. I never thought to question the dubious correlation between size of toes and witchy-hood, but just accepted what she said.

While it is not as obvious as toe size or talking to spoons, there are subtle telltale signals that can identify women who live alone. These include a lack of eye contact, dressing to be invisible, and a certain bowed, efficient brittleness. At the other end of the spectrum, there can be a slightly desperate over-compensating and over-sharing by some women who miss the contact and attention of other people. You can spot both types in a crowd. Don't join that club! We need to be vigilant that we don't tiptoe across the line into weird or transparent. We have to be our own role models, showing in our bearing and demeanour that all is well.

The fastest growing demographic in the world

We are a mighty army! There are nearly three hundred million of us globally. We are part of the biggest social trend since the rise of Baby Boomers. Two million Australians live alone (a quarter of all households) and two thirds of us prefer it that way. Solo dwellers are the fastest growing housing demographic in Australia and the Australian Institute of Family Studies predicts that by 2026 single-person households will outnumber traditional nuclear families.

This is consistent with the global trend, which has seen a rise of almost 50 per cent in the number of people living alone in the past 15 years. Today, 32 per cent of American households are single dwellers, over half of them women. A hefty half of all Manhattan homes contain people living alone. That's pipped to the post by some parts of Scandinavia, where 60 per cent of households are soloists. The rise of people living alone is not only a Western phenomenon – there is a steep rise in China and India too (albeit off a small base).

Of course, only a fraction of these are people consciously choosing the solo life. People are getting married later, we have an ageing population with spouses outliving their partners, plus those of us in the middle who are not in a relationship or are divorced. Despite the large numbers, I still feel part of an unacknowledged shadow population.

Solo dwellers account for 35 per cent of all consumer spending, so why do companies (yes, food manufacturers, supermarkets, banks, holiday companies, restaurants – I'm talking to you) ignore us? Where are the products tailored for 'ones'?

A transformational experience

Living alone can be the tip of an iceberg of transformation, a catalyst for action. It is not a shutting down of opportunities, but an opening up. The main benefits of being Han Solo are the opportunities for self-discovery and the satisfaction in completing a PhD in self-reliance. Like an archaeologist, you get to excavate the authentic you, warts and all. You find out what you like and don't like about yourself, have the time and space to work on it, think about what you want out of life and how to go about getting it.

Solo living gives you the space to imagine and curate your life, with no compromise. If you are new to it, allow yourself some time to let go of the old life, whether it was good or bad. Throw off the bowline and let yourself drift in neutral for a while as you gradually find your bearings. Then you'll be in the right space to identify some markers and move on to embrace your new personal world. It can take a while to get used to and appreciate, so don't beat yourself up if you find it hard going. We all do sometimes. It's a gradual shifting of gears.

--------------------------------- ---------------------------------

'It is the privilege of loneliness;
in privacy one may do as one chooses.'

VIRGINIA WOOLF, *MRS. DALLOWAY*

Living *by* yourself or *with* yourself?

You can't live your life believing you came second. Or mourning a parallel life that you might have led, used to have, or feel you deserved if only it hadn't slipped through your fingers like a Golden Snitch. This is your reality now, your very own House of Life, and you owe it to yourself to open every damn door and see what lies beyond. You own it. You inhabit it. It might seem just semantics, but there really is a big difference between living *by* yourself and living *with* yourself. An acceptance and a peace. It puts you on the front foot and makes you accountable.

You can make it a bento box of delights, or a Pandora's box of struggles. Same box. You make the choice, and our lives are built choice by choice. I saw one book refer to this as 'intentionality', a word that set off my bullshit antenna, but probably quite accurate. Design your life the way you want it. You can make it easy, or you can make it hard – the difference is in your mindset. And that's what the next chapter is about.

'To exist is to change, to change is to mature, to mature is to create oneself endlessly.'

HENRI BERGSON

TAKE AWAYS

Consider the times in your life
that have prepared you for living alone
- you've got this.

Revise your expectations.

Buck society's clichés of a
woman living alone.

We are part of a mighty army.

Living alone can be the catalyst
for transformation.

Live with yourself, not by yourself.

Chapter 2

MENTAL STRENGTH AND SHIFT

Tools to keep you strong ✳ *Facing up to loneliness*

Living alone is not for the faint hearted. I am inspired by the people I meet who live alone and love it. As Bette Davis famously said, 'Old age ain't no place for sissies', and neither is living alone. For all its precious gifts of time and space, living alone comes with snakes as well as ladders. We learned to 'stay calm and carry on' long before the posters told us to. Our mettle is tested every single day. Given our numbers, living alone should be The New Normal, but it doesn't feel like it. We belong to a different tribe. There are times I have felt sheet-of-glass invisible and diminished by a society where I don't seem to tick the boxes. We have to be tough, resilient and learn to dig deep. I have developed a protective carapace, but am aware there is a fine line between self-protection and coming across as brittle, finicky and defensive. It's a balancing act, and sometimes it gets to me. Just when I'm having a great day, someone might say something thoughtless in passing, oblivious to its impact, which sends me into a tailspin. It can get tiring convincing everyone (and sometimes even ourselves) that we like living alone.

The following twelve tools can help you navigate the treacherous shallows of solo living.

Tool #1 Know who you want to be

Pick three adjectives that capture who you want to be. They will change over time, but it is useful to land them, as they set a platform of values on which to base choices and actions. Some of the words might be useful for a short time when you have a specific goal to achieve. Others will stay with you for longer. It's up to you. They don't all have to be serious. If you have faced some hard times, throw in a couple of uplifting ones.

Here are some values to consider: positive, courageous, kind, capable, powerful, inspirational, calm, optimistic, wise, gentle, loving, strong, gracious, compassionate, open, efficient, friendly, active, gregarious, patient, happy, generous, passionate, disciplined, committed and caring.

Act like the person you want to be and eventually you become that person. Be the light you seek.

Tool #2 You are in control of how you react

There will be many times when you will need to call on your inner resources to be strong and brave. You have to accept that you can't outrun negative feelings, or try to push them back like King Canute with the waves. You have to confront them, or align yourself with these feelings, get to understand them better and take control from the inside out.

I speak from experience, because some nights the needling, poking fingers of doubt and fear creep into my mind in the cracks between sleep and wakefulness. I worry that I will grow ill, old and die alone and that I will not be missed. *Jane, Jane, Jane, get a grip.* When you are by yourself, your mind can run away to irrational places, down rabbit holes of Hooded Claw scariness or take flight in the sky like a runaway kite. It isn't rational, it isn't real, it isn't true, and in the cold light of day it will be fine. Remind yourself that you are in control of your thoughts, not the other way round.

It is useful to bear this in mind when people upset you. Often they are unaware of the impact of their words or actions. I tell myself it is no more than a reflection of how they feel about themselves. When you react impulsively you give your power away. When someone really upsets me, I mentally hold up a shield with a mirror on the side facing them, to protect myself and demonstrate that it is about them, not about me. One of the most useful pieces of advice given to me is that you can't affect how people act towards you, or change certain events, but *you can control how you react to them.* You can't change the direction of the wind, but you can change the direction of your sails.

✳

'People are lonely because they build
walls instead of bridges.'

JOSEPH FORT NEWTON

It is the same with living alone: you may wish you had a partner or lived in a family but the reality is that you don't, so it is how you *react* to your circumstances that determines how you enjoy your solo life. My own situation has shown me that hard times toughen you up. The grit in the oyster makes the pearl. So when things go wrong – and they will – imagine them as a series of curtains that you sweep aside to reveal a stronger, wiser you. Alternatively, just walk into the woods with a dozen eggs and pelt them against a tree with all your might – feel your anger dissipate with satisfaction!

Tool #3 Staring loneliness down

It's Good Friday morning of the Easter long weekend, and I will be completely alone for all of it. My ex has taken the children away for a 'family' trip with his girlfriend and her daughter. Ouch. Part of me is delighted to have four clear days to myself – *four whole days* – with nothing planned. There is so much that I want and need to do, not least write this book, catch up on emails, clear the decks etc. Most of me relishes the prospect, but I'd be lying to myself – and to you – if I didn't admit that there is a speck, a mote, of loneliness hanging in the air. It wriggles like a cell in a Petri dish.

'It's hard to fight an enemy who has outposts in your head.'

SALLY KEMPTON

Being *alone* is not the issue per se. It is our *minds* that create loneliness, and it wears many masks. It can present itself as sadness, apathy, listlessness, rejection, tiredness or depression. It is palpable. It is real. It is not to be dismissed lightly. How can you tackle loneliness head on?

It's normal. Surrender to it and move on

Loneliness comes with the territory. Fact. Every person I spoke to while researching this book brought up the topic of loneliness. Everyone feels it, some more, some less. It is like travelling through hilly countryside and slipping now and again into dark valleys. It is to be expected. Just don't stay there and pitch your tent. Substitute the word 'loneliness' for 'sorrow' in this quote from *Flying Solo* by Carol M. Anderson and Susan Stewart: 'You cannot prevent the birds of sorrow from flying over your head, but you can prevent them from building a nest in your hair.'

To stop it getting a grip, loneliness can be countered on two fronts: mentally and physically. The former is more powerful. Even though you can physically surround yourself with people, you know that how you feel has nothing to do with them but is a condition of self. You can't outrun it: you are only running away from yourself. So accept it, surrender to it, and deal with it. This is a process described by Susan Baumgartner in her book *My Walden*: 'Loneliness, once the captor of my spirit, now seems like a dear companion and wears the gentler name of solitude. It happened slowly, gradually. Instead of fighting loneliness, I learned to take it inside of me and to fill it with thoughts and fantasies and plans. I structured it to be productive. I learned to count on its solid presence. It seems like I am never lonely any more.'

Accept that loneliness, along with happiness, sadness, birth, death, love and rapture are part of the human condition. Then move on.

Keep loneliness in perspective

It is never as bad as it seems. Hanako was an elephant given to Japan by the government of Thailand in 1949 when she was just two. She lived in a small enclosure in Tokyo Zoo for the next 67 years and died recently *without ever seeing another elephant again*. She was dubbed 'The loneliest elephant in the world'. The reason I mention her is to put your loneliness in perspective. However lonely we are, on the 'Hanako scale' it's nothing.

Being lonely isn't about being alone

When you stop to think about it (and we rarely do), it isn't the act of being alone that makes us feel lonely. I agree with Roy Sharpe (quoted in *Celebrating Time Alone* by Lionel Fisher) who said that it is living an unproductive, self-centred, unloving, friendless life that actually makes someone feel lonely. So take control and don't make yourself a casualty of loneliness. Pick these off one by one and work on making your life productive, outward-focused and loving.

You are important

There are times when I think that no one would miss me if I disappeared in a puff of smoke. That makes me feel lonely. Rationally, I am sure they would and to remind myself I keep a big scrapbook with loving cards, letters and emails from friends and family. I am important to them. I have it in writing.

You have to have a sense of self-worth, and to like yourself. You must be important to *you*. I cover this in more detail in Chapter 3.

Don't let the fear of loneliness get to you

Franklin D. Roosevelt said, 'The only thing we have to fear is fear itself', meaning fear is a state of mind that has the power to affect us if we let it. It is not a real, physical thing but it will have an impact on our minds if we allow it to. In his book *The Eighth Passenger* Miles Tripp tells how, during the Second World War, Lancaster bomber crews consisted of seven men, but they sometimes referred to the 'eighth passenger'. This was a passenger they were all aware of and who, although invisible, would influence the outcome of their mission. That passenger was fear, and they knew they had to control it.

The *fear* of loneliness has the power to upset us more than loneliness itself, which has no capacity to harm us. Don't allow it to get a grip. Fold it up, put it in a box and throw yourself wholeheartedly into something else.

You are not alone

You are not alone in feeling lonely, because all over the world there are others feeling the same velvet sadness, and we are all connected by invisible threads. I am willing to bet that somewhere, right now, among the 300 million people (!) who live by themselves, someone will feel as you do. Take comfort in that.

'Courage is the first of human qualities because it is the quality which guarantees the others.'

ARISTOTLE

Be wary of social media

With technology you are never really alone unless you choose to be, but somehow loneliness feels more acute, painful and poignant in this switched on, screen-filled, connected society. I can't be the only person who feels pangs of – what is it: envy, sadness, FOMO? – looking at some of the more smug Facebook postings as I sit at home, alone, on a wet Saturday night. I just know that I am *not* that lucky person laughing in the bosom of a jolly family gathering, sitting with partners at that dinner, or soaking up the atmosphere in Paris, Bali or Bhutan with my husband. On balance, Facebook does not help loneliness. Block the ersatz friends and use technology proactively, Skyping or emailing friends or joining a virtual community you are interested in. Think about what social media adds to or detracts from your life and cut your cloth accordingly.

Ignore the advice on the Internet

Sometimes the Internet is invaluable. Other times, it serves us up a pile of steaming... well, you know what. When it comes to advice on countering loneliness, it's the latter. Here are some patronising suggestions that I picked off the web in five minutes, along with my commentary in brackets afterwards. Gosh, they make my blood boil.

- 'Improving social skills. Some researchers argue that loneliness is primarily the result of lacking the interpersonal skills required to create and maintain relationships.' *(Don't get me started on this one...)*
- 'Get out of the house and have fun. Perhaps you're a birdwatcher and you don't even know it yet.' *(Go on, patronise me some more, please.)*

- 'Scope out potential friends.' *(Creepy and desperate.)*
- 'Stay positive.' *(You've never been lonely, have you?)*
- 'If you are lonely, don't dwell on the fact. Get up and get out! Go somewhere where there are a lot of people. Don't worry if you don't know any of them; sometimes being around other people can help brighten your spirits.' *(Or can make you feel so much worse…)*
- 'Join a club, like a gardening club. You'll meet some mighty fine people, have fun doing work you love and learn more about gardening; plus, you'll be able to share your gardening wisdom with others… all of which will make you feel LESS lonely. *(Did you really say 'mighty fine'? Another glib sentiment trotted out by someone who has never experienced loneliness.)*
- 'Don't sit back and feel defeated. Put a smile on your face and do something different to cure your loneliness.' *(If only it were that easy, buddy.)*
  And, finally, my personal favourite:
- 'Get a pet… if Tom Hanks can live with Wilson for years you could certainly benefit from a dog or a cat. Pets can make terrific companions. Just make sure you don't substitute their company for people. Try to maintain a few human connections so that you have others to talk to and lean on in trying times.' *(So we might benefit from something more than a painted volleyball, then? The sensitivity of Attila the Hun…)*

Aaarrrggh! Patronising at best, unhelpful and incredibly insensitive at worst, written by people who have never felt the icy breath of loneliness down their necks, nor its grey mist in their homes.

Know what triggers the feeling of loneliness for you

… and develop strategies accordingly. Sometimes loneliness lances through you, triggered by a couple whispering together in a restaurant, or coming home to a dark and silent house, or going to a New Year's Eve party, or when no one meets you at the airport, or just being alone for a weekend. It's different for everyone.

Work out what makes you feel lonely, then set about developing tactics to avoid those situations, or brace yourself and deploy your anti-loneliness toolkit.

The anti-loneliness tool kit

Think of loneliness as a door that opens onto other things that will make you feel better. What's behind that door is very personal, and what works for one person won't work for another. Only you know what works for you.

Here are some thought starters:
- Access a memory that makes you feel happy to your core.
- Have a go-to book you know you will get lost in.
  (I'm quite partial to *Tintin*!)
- Identify a specific TED talk or podcast that gives you a lift.
- Go to an art gallery.
- Finish something.
- Learn something new from YouTube.
- Immerse yourself in nature as best you can. Get out to the country, or go to your local park.
- Organise some magazine subscriptions. Ignore the mainstream, airbrushed, celebrity nonsense and find smaller niche magazines

based on an interest you have, such as *Cook's Illustrated*, *Parabola*, *Dumbo Feather*, *Art Doll*, *Monocle*, *Flea Market Décor* or *Brand*. Put aside a few copies for when you're down.

- Turn to the professionals. No, not counsellors, but comedians. Find a particular comedy show that you love. It could be online, DVD or an audiobook. My favourite is the BBC radio series *Cabin Pressure*.
- Do something to help someone else: volunteer, offer someone a helping hand, or put $5 bills on strangers' windscreens with a note.
- Go for a walk you've never done before, or just do something you've never done before.
- Call a friend and tell them how you are feeling, but make sure it's a friend who knows the drill. In other words, make sure it is someone who will understand and listen to you and not just prattle on about themselves and their perfect life (which, incidentally, it rarely is). In the past I have called the wrong friend and it can do more harm than good.

Is it loneliness or depression?

Depression slinks in under your defenses. In tiny doses it can sometimes reveal unspoken truths. Once you've been touched by it you are in a much better position to help others. So I do understand the feelings of numbness, despair and worthlessness that depression

'The worst loneliness is not to be comfortable with yourself.'

MARK TWAIN

brings, and how you have to climb out from that, whether it is with a guide (a doctor or counsellor) or by reviewing your own attitudes and actions. Andrew Solomon travelled the world researching his excellent book *The Noonday Demon: An Atlas of Depression* and came to the conclusion that the opposite of depression is not happiness, but *vitality* – taking action. It can be hard to tackle depression alone and friends are not always the best people to help, as they lack training and don't want to fall into the sinkhole with you. If you need professional help, reach out and get it.

Tool #4 Shift from 'loneliness' to 'solitude'

Paul Tillich wrote: 'Our language has wisely sensed the two sides of being alone. It has created the word "loneliness" to express the pain of being alone. And it has created the word "solitude" to express the glory of being alone.'

Turn your back on loneliness with its judgement and isolation and turn towards its more welcoming sister, solitude. Solitude brings with it a sense of choice and pride. You choose to partake in solitude, whereas loneliness is thrust upon you, so do a Rumpelstiltskin and spin the straw of loneliness into the gold of solitude. An old Buddhist scripture says, 'A tenth of an inch difference and heaven and earth are set apart'. Solitude and loneliness might also be separated by a tenth of an inch, but it's enough to make them different.

'Have patience and shuffle the cards.'

MIGUEL DE CERVANTES

Sarah Holbrook chose to embrace her solitude in an extreme way, selling her house and business and moving to a cabin in the woods in rural America. In *Celebrating Time Alone* by Lionel Fisher she talks of how she chose to accept and face her aloneness as a wonderful, precious secret, rather than being scared of it.

You need to make a number of conscious mental shifts when you live alone, and this is one of them. Don't ever think of living alone as a sentence to be served. Shift your perspective. Reimagine it. Solitude is not a weighty albatross round your neck. Let it embrace you, and wrap its protective wings around you. It is a means to an end. Solitude rewards you if you listen.

Tool #5 Happiness on purpose

'If you want to be happy, be,' said Tolstoy. He was on to something long before Harvard had its Happiness Centre and books like *The Happiness Advantage* and *The Happiness Project* captured our imaginations. The world is as you perceive it. So, if you feel that you've missed out, or that the hand you've been dealt is unfair, that is your reality. I am not glibly

'Often people attempt to live their lives backwards: they try to have more things, or more money in order to do more of what they want, so they will be happier. The way it works is actually the reverse. You must first be who you really are, then do what you need to do, in order to have what you want.'

MARGARET YOUNG

saying Think Positive with an annoying smiley face emoji, but research (and common sense) shows that a positive mindset leads to positive outcomes. Think about how you want to frame your day as soon as your feet touch the floor in the morning. The experts have proven that it is happiness that makes you successful, not the other way round.

In his book *The Seven Secrets of Happiness* British broadcaster Gyles Brandreth identified these rules. You can't pick and choose, he warns... You have to live by all of them. The rules are:

One: Cultivate a passion

Two: Be a leaf of a tree (Be an individual but connected to a bigger community)

Three: Break the mirror – avoid narcissism

Four: Don't resist change – embrace the new

Five: Audit your happiness. If you spend more than half your time doing something you don't enjoy, do something about it.

Six: Live in the moment. Relish what's happening now and don't worry too much about the future

Seven: Be happy. 'Choose to be optimistic,' says the Dalai Lama. 'It feels better.'

Dr. Martin Seligman in his turn suggests five factors that contribute to happiness: positive emotion and pleasure, achievement, relationships, engagement and meaning. The last two are the most important. If we are engaged in what we do and find ways to make our lives more meaningful, happiness will show up as a byproduct.

Dr. Tim Sharp (aka 'Dr. Happy') has seven pointers: nurture relationships, look ahead, use your strengths, be healthy, look on the bright side, be thankful and forgive, and create purpose. I am a realist and do not expect my life to be wall-to-wall happiness. I'm just asking for a few fun-sized potato chip bags of the stuff and I appreciate it's up to me. We are all walking mirrors, so even though it might take a while to deploy some of these strategies, just adopting an optimistic outlook will attract similar.

Tool #6 Toughen up with a totem

We soloists are trapeze artists without a safety net. Criticism and hurtful comments can quickly knock us off balance, and I am constantly surprised and disappointed by how many of those there can be. Some come from strangers, others from friends or frenemies. Most of these people don't live by themselves and don't have an inkling of how they hurt us. That's fine; life goes on. Without being Pollyanna-ish about it, hard times have a way of offering an opportunity for growth, even if it takes years to learn the lesson. Maybe for them as well.

We have to develop a thick skin. Wrap yourself in a metaphorical cloak and watch the hurt repelled. I have learned lessons in resilience from three wild animals and have adopted them as my unofficial totems.

They are a special wild dog, a lioness and a bison.

'If we all threw our problems in a pile and saw everybody else's, we'd grab ours back.'

REGINA BRETT

Solo the Wild Dog

When I was a child I was given a book called *Solo* by Hugo van Lawick. It is about an African wild dog puppy, the runt, whose siblings were killed by another dog. Solo is picked on and struggles to keep up with the pack while they ignore her, but she never, ever gives up. (You can see how the story ends in wildfilmhistory.org under Hugo van Lawick and The Wild Dogs of Africa). I love the image of Solo with her bright eyes, and her ears torn by the other dogs, the epitome of resilience. Her example stuck with me.

A Lioness

When I was in the process of getting divorced, one image had a profound impact on me. It was from a bas-relief in the British Museum of an Assyrian lioness, badly wounded but still fighting. Now I see myself as a lone lioness, strength regained, self-contained and proud.

A Bison

Here's an interesting fact. When a bad snowstorm hits, bison are the only creatures that instinctively turn around and walk *into* it, knowing it is the quickest way through. Maybe I am getting anthropomorphically carried away, but you've got to love an animal that confronts its hardships head on, no flinching.

Solo's persistence, the lioness' desperate resilience and the bison's ability to confront things directly remind me to stay strong against naysayers, backbiters and frenemies, the lot of them.

Tool #7 Turn your adventure of living alone into a project

Why not write about or document your story of living alone? What works? What advice would you give to others? What have been the disasters and what have you learned from them? What was the process of getting rid of the 'l' in 'alone' and turning it into 'a one'?

There are several women who have written about living alone, including Joan Anderson (*A Year By the Sea*), Anne Morrow Lindbergh (*Gift from the Sea*), and Alix Kates Shulman (*Drinking the Rain*). Read them for more inspiration.

Living alone well is a state of mind that has to be cultivated. Explore it as you would a new country and draw a map of your life by yourself as an island. What are the good parts and what are the challenging parts? What are the beautiful parts you are proud of? Which parts are still unexplored?

Tool #8 Be kind to yourself

As women, we are very tough on ourselves and I think living alone exacerbates this. I feel like the king pole – the centre pole of the big top – responsible for holding everything up and sometimes not doing a very good job of it. We ask so much of ourselves and when we fall short it knocks our self-esteem.

Not everyone does amazing things. Just doing one thing suggested in this book puts you ahead of the pack. So don't think about anyone else, congratulate yourself on what you have done and don't fret about what you have yet to achieve. It will happen. Everyone's journey is different.

Tool #9 Find your *ikigai* - your purpose

'Tell me, what is it you plan to do with your one wild and precious life?' asked American poet Mary Oliver.

In Japanese culture, everyone has an *ikigai*, or reason to get up in the morning. It's a healthy passion for something that makes us feel life is worth living; a purpose, in other words. Finding or, more accurately, unearthing it helps give you direction, like putting a destination into Google Maps.

I would thoroughly recommend the book *Finding Your Element: How to discover your talents and passions and transform your life* by Ken Robinson, which offers several practical techniques and tools to nail your 'element' or purpose. It is split into 10 chapters:

1. Finding Your Element
2. What are you good at?
3. How do you know?
4. What do you love?
5. What makes you happy?
6. What's your attitude?
7. Where are you now?
8. Where's your tribe?
9. What's Next?
10. Living a Life of Passion and Purpose

By the time you have completed all the exercises I guarantee you'll be the closest you ever have to pinpointing your *ikigai*.

If 'Finding Your Purpose' sounds too daunting a task and you aren't drawn to it, that's fine. Not all of us have a huge mission. In their book *The ONE Thing*, authors Gary Keller and Jay Papasan advise: 'Think of it simply as the ONE thing you want your life to be about more than any other. Try writing down something you'd like to accomplish and then describe how you'd do it … Pick a direction, start marching down that path, and see how you like it. Time brings clarity and if you find you don't like it, you can always change your mind. It's your life.'

There are many threads of experience in our lives that can point us towards our purpose. Sometimes it is already present in our lives in some way, but may be on the periphery, or in the past. Lift up the top of your mind, grab some chopsticks, and have a poke around. Don't feel it has to be Big and Grand. It might not be. Just right for you. It will come to you; there's no need to chase too hard. Life speaks to us all the time; there are often clues. Our job is to listen.

Tool #10 Be your own good company, motivator and cheerleader

You are Team Jane, or Team Sarah or Team whatever your name is. A team of one. You spend more time with yourself than anyone else, so make sure you are good company. I am lucky enough to enjoy my own company, but if you don't enjoy yours, what can you do to make it better?

People rarely give compliments or praise, so fill the vacuum yourself. Don't wait for others to say 'well done' or 'good for you'. Pat yourself on the back regularly. You are doing so well just putting one foot in front of another.

Tool #11 Slam the door in negativity's face

Nora's door slam at the end of Ibsen's *A Doll's House* is a famous moment in the history of theatre. It was called 'The door slam heard around the

'Very little is needed to make a happy life; it is all within yourself, in your way of thinking.'

MARCUS AURELIUS

world' and is a metaphor for Nora finding her independence and putting her unsatisfactory marriage behind her (very unusual at a time when women were expected to be submissive to men). We need to acknowledge negative thoughts, even naming them if that helps. 'You are pettiness'; 'you are impatience'; 'you are frustration'. Then we have to be as firm as Nora about slamming the door on them.

Instead of whining about how and why you are in a particular situation, find the nearest reflective surface and work out what you're going to do about it. 'When you are complaining, you become a living, breathing crap magnet' as T. Harv Eker memorably put it. He challenges us to not complain at all for seven days and see how it changes your life. Being a victim might get you attention in the short term, but it won't get you friends or success in the long run.

Of course things get tough. I don't live in Pretendy Land. My heart still contracts a little when I hear myself squeaking a thank you at the supermarket checkout, not having spoken to a soul all day. Or I wake up at night, crushed under a wall of worry, missing the comfort of knowing that someone has my back.

No thought lives in your head rent-free and negative thoughts take their toll. They whisper in your ear: 'You're old; you're not attractive; you're a failure; you're overweight; how could anyone love you?; What do you contribute to the world?' It is ridiculous, given how strong women inherently are, that we are in thrall to these whining voices. Repel and rebuff them with a dynamic force. We need to diminish their power or they will establish a stronghold. Avoid developing a habit of discontent, which is an emotional cul de sac. Pull yourself out of it, wring the shipwreck water out of your hair and carry on. You choose the thoughts that circulate in your mind.

Here are some ways to stop the negative soundtrack:

- If you have a grievance, tell someone about it, just once, then go for a walk, meditate and/or write it in your journal or on a piece of paper and tear it up or burn it, then let it go. Don't keep complaining. No one is interested.
- Just tell yourself to stop it.
- Do something, however small, that notches you towards your goals.
- Accept that what you worry about in the middle of the night is irrational and in the light of day is manageable.
- Distraction. List the names of all of your friends, your favourite books, a poem you've learned – anything.
- Seek out the company of a positive friend (a 'radiator' not a 'drain').
- Reimagine the problem, and focus on the positives within it.
- Know that negative things are not permanent.
- Imagine someone else saying what you're thinking. How would you react?
- Help someone else.
- Write down your strengths.
- Make a file of positive music. A couple of my favourites are 'Praan' by Garry Schyman and 'On Earth as it is in Heaven' from *The Mission* soundtrack by Ennio Morricone. Play it loudly!

Say to yourself, as does the Broadway star Sierra Boggess: 'You are enough. You are so enough. It's unbelievable how enough you are.'

Tool #12 Act 'as if'

The words we choose have a powerful impact on how we feel, the way we approach things, and the outcome. The more you say: 'I want…' or 'I need…' the less likely you are to get it. Instead, act as if it's already happened and you're reaping the benefits. So, replace 'I *wish I was* successful' with 'I *am* successful' and 'I *wish* I had a job I liked' with 'I *have* a fulfilling job', and then act accordingly. You'll notice a remarkable difference in your attitude straight away. This frame of mind is much more likely to lead to success.

I know, because I had to find a full-time job, in my fifties, and now I have to find another one. My negative voice whispers, 'I'm too old, no one will hire me'. I recognise that it is a self-fulfilling prophecy, so have replaced it with, 'I am already adding value to the clients I work with. I am calmly confident in my ability and have meaningful experience to offer'. Still, sitting at home with a positive attitude reading *The Secret* and eating crumpets won't get me a job. Shaking the network tree and sending out my CV with a cracking cover letter will. I now approach it with confidence and act 'as if'.

'You gain strength, courage and confidence by every experience in which you really stop to look fear in the face … You must do the thing you think you cannot do.'

ELEANOR ROOSEVELT

Alternatively, if acting 'as if' doesn't come naturally, reframe the negative issues into positive, practical 'how can I fix this?' questions.

'I can't afford it' becomes 'How can I afford it?'

'I can't' becomes 'How can I?'

'I'm finding it hard' becomes 'I'm working towards'.

'I should' becomes 'I will'.

… you get the idea.

Try playing Positive Word Bingo. Write down half a dozen positive words and make sure to get them into your conversations or emails for the rest of the day.

This too shall pass

When things threaten to overwhelm and you feel your little solo rowing boat is taking on water, keep things in perspective. Whatever troubles you are going through only represent a tiny dot on your line of life. In one year, or five, it will matter less, or not at all. You are stronger than you think.

TAKE AWAYS

Living alone requires enormous amounts of
mental strength. Luckily we have it.

Know who you want to be (three adjectives).

You are in control of how you react.

Stare loneliness down.

Shift from 'loneliness' to 'solitude'.

Be happy on purpose.

Toughen up with a totem
(a wild dog, a lioness, a bison).

Turn your adventure of living alone
into a project.

Be kind to yourself.

Find your *ikigai*.

Be your own good company, motivator
and cheerleader.

Slam the door in negativity's face.

Act 'as if' it has already happened.

Chapter 3

RELATIONSHIPS

*Yourself * Family * Friends * Romance*
** Community * Four-legged creatures*

I am sure I am not the only person living alone who occasionally wonders, if I fell down a manhole, how long it would take anyone to notice I'd disappeared. Ridiculous really; but not a bad litmus test to see how connected (or not) you are to others. Or feel you are.

We all want to be loved (and noticed, and missed, in the manhole scenario) but when you live alone your solar system of relationships is different to other people's. It shifts more, with some relationships coming into the foreground as others recede – and they are not always the ones you expect. You realise the importance of friends and relatives, not least as a safety net, when sometimes they are all that lies between you and the drop below. I feel like a pendulum, swinging backwards and forwards between my love of solitude and the pull towards companionship, love, laughter and the occasional intimate touch.

Ironically, the skills that make us good at living alone also make us great to be around. Research has clearly shown that people who live alone are more sociable than those who live with other people. As Albert Guinon said, 'People who cannot bear to be alone are generally the worst company'.

Relationships tend to be magnifiers of emotions. Being alone has made me more discerning than ever about who plays a role my life. By that I don't mean to imply that someone is lucky to be my friend. What I do mean is that anyone who makes me feel bad and doubt myself does not belong in my (oh so precious) life.

Relationships ranked in order of importance for those who live alone:

1. Yourself
2. Family
3. Friends
4. Romance
5. Your 'village'

'Your task is not to seek love but merely
to seek and find all the barriers within yourself
that you have built against it.'

RUMI

1.
Yourself

It's the most important relationship in the world: the one you have with yourself. You're the one. When you live alone it is crucial that you like what you see when you look in the mirror. Not your physical body, but your spirit and who you are. What your eyes say about you.

Imagine meeting someone you immediately feel a connection with; someone who completely gets your fears and dreams. Someone who's funny and great company and inspirational. A person you'd like to spend time with. It's you! Until you love that person (and it is 'until', not 'unless'), nothing else will fall into place. Like yourself and you'll never be lonely. (It's also a prerequisite for anyone else to love you back.)

They say that 'the entire sum of existence is the magic of being needed by just one person'. Sometimes that person needs to be you.

The way to be happy is to develop an unshakeable sense of self-worth. It's easier said than done, as most of us judge ourselves very harshly. Rate yourself from one to 10, with 10 as complete acceptance and self-belief and one as self-rejection. What's your number? You've got to push yourself up that scale because low self-esteem can bleed into all your relationships.

The self-help industry makes millions from women who are dissatisfied with themselves. Change the script from 'there are lots of things I'd change about myself, plus a few good bits' to 'I am basically good and there are a few bits I'm working on'. If you don't like yourself, no one else will. I love Suze Orman's joyous comment: 'I'd date myself!' Once you have that confidence and power, no one can take it away from you. There's a line in Liane Moriarty's *What Alice Forgot* that jumped out at me: 'It's not actually possible for a dried apricot to shine.' So plump yourself up.

So far, so predictable. 'Yup,' I can hear you thinking, 'No shit, Sherlock'. But how exactly do you go about liking yourself more and acquiring that self-confidence that leads to greater self-esteem and self-worth? Try these on for size:

a) Be a friend to yourself

The conversations you have in your head are the most powerful you'll ever have. We have 50,000 thoughts a day, so make sure they're kind ones. We are all familiar with the negative dialogue that can run around inside our heads. Imagine if you spoke to a friend that way: the friendship wouldn't last long. So speak to yourself as a good friend would, or an alter ego (give her a name if you want) and feel the shift straight away. If you have the capacity to love someone else, you have the capacity to love yourself.

Christopher Germer expressed it perfectly: 'A moment of self-compassion can change your entire day. A string of such moments can change the course of your life.'

b) Don't be so hard on yourself

We set ourselves ridiculously high expectations and then beat ourselves up when we don't meet them. Imagine you're a show jumper: get off your horse, go around the course and lower the height of all the jumps. Doesn't that feel better? This is not about dumbing down, but about being realistic. Don't get dragged down by the anchor of self-blame or self-doubt. Replace your mile-long 'to do' list with a 'done' list and watch your levels of satisfaction rise. Living alone already gives you a head start in the productivity stakes, and each notch you make towards your goals will increase your sense of self-worth exponentially, so don't set the bar too high. It is not an expectation to live up to, as much as a possibility to *live into*.

c) Keep a self-esteem scrapbook

I keep a scrapbook filled with the positive letters, cards and emails that friends (and readers!) have sent. These include thank you notes, and supportive letters when my marriage ended, through to scraps of paper when my book-club girls wrote down three adjectives that captured each of our personalities. On grey days, when colour is rationed and I feel that being alone is a euphemism for being flawed, it's amazing what a boost it is to read them.

On the first page I have written a list of positive things about myself. (As someone who is instinctively self-deprecating, that was not an easy task.) Write your own and read them out loud. Or email them to yourself. If a positive mantra works for you, add that in too.

'Set your life on fire. Seek those who fan the flames.'

RUMI

d) Hold your defining image

Imagine how you look at your happiest: an image that captures your inner essence; a reflection of how you want to see yourself, not distorted by the perceptions of others, like in a fairground House of Mirrors. It could be a photograph of you laughing with friends, or walking along a beach, or looking out to sea. It could be a real photo or just an image in your head, but it should help remind you of the great soul you are, especially on dark days when you might be walking in tar and feel emotionally mugged.

e) Identify the essence of you

When you live alone you are given a wonderful opportunity to explore who you are and what you're made of. Anneli Rufus, in her book *Unworthy*, explores how to dismantle some self-esteem booby traps: 'Your post-self-loathing self is not some total stranger. He or she is you, the true you, found again. We might not find our post-self-loathing selves in magazines, waving to us from fashion spreads, but we can "hear" our true "languages" in books, films, pictures, nature, music, laughter: wherever real or pretend people are. Make it a game – a sacred secret game. What "speaks" to you? Names? Colours? Landscapes? Lines of dialogue? Each is a starting point. Each is a tiny light.'

Again, if it helps, keep a scrapbook (digital or physical) of images that give you a visceral response and capture the wonderful things that make up you. Your 'Jane-ness' or 'Kate-ness' or 'Sarah-ness'. Maybe give yourself a trademark or two that captures it – perhaps always wearing a flower in your hair, a slash of red lipstick, holding a special dinner party on the same date every year, or wearing unique jewellery.

f) Ditch regrets and blame

You choose to be Velcro or Teflon. You can attract and keep hold of worries, or just let them slip off you. We all have them – regrets, blame, misgivings – but they serve no purpose in our lives. They throw hooks into us and try to pull us back. So unhitch yourself, whip off your Regrets & Blame t-shirt, take a step forwards and accept full responsibility for your life. Even if you feel strongly that someone has wronged you, *you* are responsible for your reactions and your response. Don't look backwards, only forwards, and feel the lightness descend and the sun sleep like an angel on your back.

As Suze Orman said: 'We are free to move forward only when we remove the emotional shackles of regret.'

g) Acquire a new skill

Try something you've never tried before. Just learn one new thing a year – a language, boxing, opera appreciation, salsa dancing. I'm having a crack at calligraphy – hardly the wisest choice for the least patient of people but it's amazing how good it makes me feel. And with YouTube you have no excuse: you can learn absolutely *everything* on YouTube. And I mean *everything*.

h) Set yourself a goal and accomplish it

You can do it. Whether it's losing five kilograms, walking 10,000 steps a day for a month, eating five portions of fruit and vegetables every day or getting a new job, set yourself a goal and then kick it into touch. This is a 100 per cent guaranteed way to have you high-fiving your reflection.

i) Celebrate your birthday

A few years ago, I had a sad panda birthday. No one remembered it, not even my children. I found myself telling people in shops, just to hear the words 'Happy Birthday'. It was pretty desperate, but never again. Now I have a two-pronged plan of attack. One: I invest in a treat day by myself – a spa, movie, my favourite restaurant for lunch – just doing something lovely, including buying myself flowers and a present. Two: I have friends over for dinner on or near the date, telling them that it is my birthday (no need for gifts). I have done this for the last couple of years and the day has been good. The trick is to plan, not leave it to chance.

A cautionary note: self-esteem or self-absorption?

Keep an eye out to ensure that your positive 'self-keeping' doesn't teeter into self-absorption or dreary narcissism. Too much focus on yourself and ongoing, over-earnest self-improvement can make you boring, so keep it in perspective. On the other hand, remember that doing something for yourself isn't necessarily selfish. In Mandarin, the word 'selfish' has two translations: 'doing something greedy' and 'doing something that benefits yourself'. We don't have that generous distinction in English, so don't feel guilty.

'Be thine own palace or the world's thy jail.'

JOHN DONNE

2.
FAMILY

I am in a tight braid of three with my two children, but have no other immediate family left, so I find it sad when people don't make an effort with their relatives. You are so lucky to have them! We are all strands within some sort of a family knot, however loose or dysfunctional, and of course there will be ups and downs. I plead guilty as I hadn't spoken to my sister for a year before she died – something I regret and have to live with – so if you are lucky enough to have siblings and close relatives, make an effort to find common ground. In recent years I have become closer to my cousins in South Africa; cousins is a great relationship, you are usually similar in age but are tied by blood, so closer than just friends.

It is possible, even probable, that some of your relations will feel it is 'sad' that you live alone, and pity you. While you must be true to yourself, make an effort to show them your best face: be a poster girl for the rest of us and demonstrate the positive aspects of your solo life. Don't let them feel sorry for you; you want positive interactions, not concerned 'Are you ok?' conversations on a loop.

When your parents die you feel more alone than ever. You can initially surrender yourself to the grief, but after a while you just have to sit alongside it. That said, not a day goes by when I don't think of my mother and father and when their voices come back to me, winnowed from memory, my chest thickens involuntarily. On Mother's Day, British comedian Sarah Millican posted this on Facebook, and had the most overwhelming response: '*Hugs to all of those who find Mother's Day a struggle. Whether you don't get on, she's no longer here, or whatever your story, I'm sending love. x*' You nailed it, Sarah.

I regret not having asked my parents more about their childhoods and courtship, the family tree and special memories. Do not follow my example! As I get older, I grow more interested in ancestry. Sometimes the past lays down markers for the future. Learning more about your family can give you a powerful understanding of why you think and feel the way you do.

Of course families are messy and don't always work out the way you'd like. A close relative of my ex-husband rejected outright my overtures of friendship after our divorce. I was hurt, but I had tried, and have now just let it go. The right people tend to come into your life at the right time, so why bother feeding the hand that bites you?

'Be kind whenever possible.
It is always possible.'

TENZIN GYASTO, 14TH DALAI LAMA

3.
FRIENDS

When I looked up the word 'alone' in my laptop's thesaurus, one of the definitions was: '*Klein felt terribly alone:* lonely, isolated, solitary, deserted, abandoned, forsaken, forlorn, friendless. Antonyms: loved, wanted, among friends.' It's interesting that the opposite of 'alone' (well at least in Klein's case) is defined as 'among friends'. I spend a lot of time alone, but never feel friendless, because I know an army of allies have my back. Friends are a gift you give yourself and when you live alone they get pushed higher up your personal totem pole of relationships. You are the average of the five people you spend most time with, so make sure they reflect who you want to be.

Be discerning

Friends are your safety net, your sounding board, your social life, a source of happiness and the underpinners of your self-worth. Friendships are like gardens – they need to be tended and cared for to thrive. But they also need to be weeded, so if you have friends who do not make you feel good about yourself, grab some pesticide.

Sometimes we outgrow people. We learn and expand, our attitudes and circumstances shift, and sometimes we just don't have much in common any more. I am not as close to some old friends as to people I have met within the last year, simply because at this point our Venn diagrams intersect. Friendships naturally ebb and flow, with a few constants we can count on.

Some 'frenemies' like to think they are helping you, but their negativity can have a disproportionate impact. An unkind word or a negative *passo agresso* comment can be a spear to the guts. I was recently hurt by a friend's thoughtless personal comments (he assumed he was being helpful) and I called him out on it. Our friendship is definitely bruised, possibly finished, but I am glad I stood my ground. Sometimes people need to be told when they have crossed the line. What you permit, you endorse. And you should not put up with friends who think along the same lines as Gore Vidal: 'Whenever a friend succeeds, a little something in me dies.'

Getting divorced or being widowed throws friendships into sharp relief. Shorn of the status of being married, most women (myself included) find that some friends distance themselves, consciously or not. You can almost hear the tectonic plates of friendship shifting and grinding as your social status is recalibrated. Sometimes you have to spell out to your friends that you'd like to be included in social events when their mental checklist of invitees doesn't seem to extend beyond couples. A married friend recently was rabbiting on about her hectic social weekend – it came as a surprise when I told her I hadn't spoken to anyone for 48 hours.

Friends might feel sympathy for your situation, but struggle to show empathy. Empathy takes work. Empathy beats sympathy. Sympathy reacts to the force it encounters – clicking and clacking, backwards and forwards, like the silver balls in a Newton's cradle. Authentic friends empathise. They walk in your shoes, they stand alongside you and they will march into battle with you. As Francis Bacon put it: 'The worst solitude is to be destitute of sincere friendship.' Sincere friends are empathetic friends.

Ways to maintain momentum in friendships

- Write a list of all of your friends and acquaintances. Prioritise those you need to pay more attention to.

- Try to send regular emails and even the occasional hand-written letter to friends who live far away. I try to write one email every quarter, and cut and paste it to personalise each one. It takes a long time, but it is worth it.

- When someone is having a tough time – especially if they've stuffed up – reach out and let them know you have their back. They will never forget it.

- Put yourself on the mailing list of theatres and galleries to be first to know when an event is coming up. When you see something you like the look of, call a few friends to check dates and then book tickets – everyone will be so happy that you did. Every summer I book several tickets to an open-air cinema and then throw open the invitations to my friends. It is always a great success.

- I enjoy cooking and try to have friends round for supper once a month. I theme the meal around a particular type of cuisine – we've had Malaysian, Persian, Korean and more.

- Go exploring! I love to explore different parts of my own city, especially the ethnic neighbourhoods. Sometimes I take friends on mini tours. I have another 'exploring' friend and finding the secret places right at our back door has proven to be a great way to bring us closer.

- When a friend comes to you with a problem, experience has taught me that rather than blurt out your thoughts on the solution, you could imagine yourself to be like water: fluid, non-judgemental, still and reflective, and help them discover the best solution themself. The Persian mystic poet Hafiz wrote 'Troubled? Then stay with me, for I am not'. And the oh-so-articulate Martha Beck said that problem solving is about simply allowing someone to be quiet enough to hear their true self.

- If you have friends who live overseas, try to include them on a holiday itinerary. On a trip to Europe I caught up with my oldest friend, HB, who lives in Brussels. I was only there for one night, but it felt so good to blow on the embers of our friendship. This is part of the email she sent me afterwards:

'Just too tantalising to have you there and to then have to say goodbye. But as I said: I am always there, you are always there, even if we are on the other side of the world. Some bonds transgress time and space. Call it love.'

Making new friends

It will come as no surprise that studies have shown people who live alone are more socially engaged than couples. One happily married friend freely admits she's 'not hiring' new friends. I admire her honesty and chutzpah, but am uncertain she'd feel the same if she were alone. We have to make an effort. I am not particularly on the look out for new friends either, but as my time living alone has stretched from months to years, I have found myself forging new friendships in lots of different places – at a French conversation class, working at a charity, with a neighbour opposite, and taking the dog for a walk around the block (our leads became entwined). Many of my new friends also happen to live alone – it's good to have a posse of positive fellow singletons who provide ballast and you might take the opportunity to redesign your inner circle. The point is that if you want to make new friends (and I would recommend it) then you have to get out there. Meetup.com is another great place to start.

When things go wrong

You learn to have a pretty thick skin, don't you? I am getting better at being on the pointy end of criticism but, with no one to download to, it still stings. I try to be Armadillo Woman and not let it pierce me. One of my most surprising disappointments was when some friends pretty much ignored me after I got divorced and started living alone. It was as if I'd been struck off a secret social register. Certainly my divorce had unsettled friends who knew their relationships were in even worse shape than mine. Grown women made me feel like Typhoid Mary. You might also learn that people who need people feel threatened by people who don't. Be strong. These 'friends' have not earned a place in your life.

I hate arguing with friends and do my best to avoid it, but sometimes it happens. Many quarrels are the result of a misunderstanding or if one person feels no one is listening. It comes down to self-validation:

---- ✳ ----

'One true friend adds more to our happiness than a thousand enemies add to our unhappiness.'

MARIE VON EBNER-ESCHENBACH

your adversary needs to know that you see them, you hear them and that what they say matters to you. Be patient, and consider them an E.G.R. – 'Extra Grace Required'. Remember that whenever you point at someone, three fingers are pointing back at you. Do you want to be right, or do you want peace? Don't let things fester. Try to resolve problems, but if you can't, walk away. Your life is too precious to have negative energy in it, or to get trapped down an emotional cul de sac. Slip out of the relationship like a snake leaving its skin behind.

Sometimes people around you will behave badly. I have learned that it's not worth wasting your energy responding to, criticising or commenting on their behaviour. Re-frame their actions as a lesson in how *not* to behave. Write down everything you want to say to them, pouring out your wounded heart, then tear it up and move on. If you hit back, judge and bitch about them, you become what they are. The author Byron Katie said, 'I am what I believe you to be in the moment that I believe it'. Maybe you have been guilty of the same behaviour? If so, rise above.

* A final thought on friends *

'There comes a point in your life when you realise: Who matters, Who never did, Who won't any more, and Who always will. So don't worry about people from your past – there's a reason why they didn't make it to your future.'

ADAM LINDSAY GORDON

4.
ROMANCE

The love between my ex-husband and me disappeared when we weren't looking. It's not easy to have a broken heart – *un coeur brisé*, or 'shattered heart', as the French say – but I learned you simply have to let old stuff go and not look back. You don't want to be the one with a heart full of splinters, even when the person you loved and trusted turns out not to be the person you thought they were. That person no longer exists… And it helps. Forgiveness is not about them; it's about you. If you don't forgive someone, your stored hatred and angst does *you* much more harm than it does them. What's worse is that it binds you to them. When you forgive someone, you release their power over you. In their book *From Age-ing to Sage-ing* authors Zalman Schacter-Shalomi and Ronald Miller have these fantastically resonating words about forgiveness:

'When I refuse to forgive someone who has wronged me, I mobilise my own inner criminal justice system to punish the offender. As judge and jury, I sentence the person to a long prison term without pardon and incarcerate him in a prison that I construct from bricks and mortar of a hardened heart. Now as jailor and warden, I must spend as much time in prison as the person I am guarding. All the energy that I put into maintaining the prison system comes out of my "energy budget". From this point of view, bearing a grudge is very "costly", because long-held feelings of anger, resentment and fear drain my energy and imprison my vitality and creativity.'

Holding on to anger is like taking poison and hoping someone else will die. It stews your organs. Steve Harvey nailed it when he said, 'You can be happy or you can be right'. (Although I can't help but laugh with a friend whose deeply flawed ex is called Rick. Or 'Rick with the silent P' as she still refers to him…)

Together, alone

I was as surprised as anyone to learn that love can spit, and that when it does it spits venom in your eye. I know what it's like to tether yourself to someone, then have your heart ripped from its moorings. It bloody hurts, even if you know that you were opposing forces – you as alkaline to their acid. But you can't drag around the corpse of a dying relationship behind you. Always remember how much better off you are alone than as one of those married couples living in a vast Sahara, a veritable Gobi Desert, of unions. Shockingly, only 25 per cent of married Australians describe their marriages as happy.

Better to be alone than wish you were. There are many people who feel utterly alone even though they live with someone. To be in a relationship characterised by indifference is the worst kind of

'It's far better to be unhappy alone than unhappy with someone — so far.'

MARILYN MONROE

'alone-ness'. Indifference, not hate, is the opposite of love, and it is awful to see how many people feel lonely within a fractured marriage or a hobbled relationship, the tentacles of the past being the only things binding them together. If you are in this situation, I hope you can find the confidence to make a break for it. Living a life of self-determination brings freedom. You should never have to justify leaving; but you do have to justify staying. If it helps, write down everything you weren't happy with in the relationship and take comfort in the fact that you will never have to deal with them again.

Although I now carry a fault line through my heart, I don't regret being married. But I know now that being married is not the only way to feel complete. You can feel complete alone.

Do. Not. Let. Anyone. Take. Away. Your. Joy.

Accepting being single

How the world misses Nora Ephron's wit and wisdom: 'It seemed to me that the desire to get married – which, I regret to say, I believe is fundamental and primal in women – is followed almost immediately

'We all have a better guide in ourselves, if we would attend to it, than any other person can be.'

JANE AUSTEN

by an equally fundamental and primal urge, which is to be single again.' On the whole, Living Alone and Being Single are pretty good companions, though it is better if they are a conscious choice, not a forced compromise.

In her book *Living Solo* Nancy Goldner distinguishes between being 'circumstantially single' and 'emotionally single'. The former means that life didn't necessarily turn out as you expected and you remain single but don't dwell on it. That's where I am. It has been a while since I wrote 'heart = stolen' in my diary. Being 'emotionally single', on the other hand, means you feel a keen sense of despair and sadness about being single, accompanied by a damaging belief that you are not entitled to get what you want out of life. This can be quite debilitating and you might require professional help to shift gears.

Feeling good about yourself as a single person does not always come easily or naturally. Society has dictated that we act in a certain way: catch the golden ring of marriage, or accept the badge of failure. If you were wanted and desirable, you wouldn't be alone, would you? Luckily, I have enough self-worth not to subscribe to these thoughts, but I face up to the real possibility that I might be alone forever. It is

'It ain't what they call you.
It's what you answer to.'

W.C. FIELDS

a common story. Among my divorced friends, *every* ex-husband has re-partnered, and quickly, but the women have not. The odds are not stacked in our favour.

Once you have been alone for a while and things begin to fall into place, you start to appreciate it more and more and wonder if the benefits of being alone (doing what I like, when I like, where I like, how I like and with whom I please) could ever be relinquished.

Romance. Do you want it?

'You'll meet someone when you least expect it.' If one more person tells me that, I will bop them on the nose; just watch me. Romance seems to be the happy ending everyone else wants for me. I'm not sure *Eat, Pray, Love* would have reached the same dizzy heights of success if it had been *Eat, Pray, Make New Friends*.

You need to decide if you are ready or willing to embark on a new relationship. If you are, you will positively exude the 'I'm up for it' vibe, which will be picked up like iron filings on a magnet by the right person, who will be in a similar frame of mind. That's how it works.

I love being alone – perhaps a bit too much – and am wary about putting myself in a position where I can be hurt again. (Or be seen naked, come to that. 'My, what big underpants you have, Jane.') Right now, my heart is silted up, curled up like the cello-end of a fern. But I know I must be careful not to shut myself down to the possibility and of course it can be wonderful to meet someone who respects the preciousness and trust inherent in an intimate relationship, and who wants you to grow and reach your full potential. And I'd love to move my sex life on from its current Halley's Comet trajectory (making a fuzzy appearance once every 75 years), although there is a comfort in celibacy. In his wonderful essay 'Going It Alone', Fenton Johnson calls it a 'joyous turning inwards' and quotes the notoriously celibate Emily Dickinson: 'Inebriate of air am I/ And a Debauchee of Dew.'

You start to wonder if it's sex you miss, or the before and after bits. Meanwhile, I am happily indulging my sensual side with candlelit baths, massages and zillion thread-count sheets. There is an audible crackle when I get into bed. And – how lucky am I? – a friend has given me a 'boyfriend pillow', in the shape of a man's headless torso, wearing (bewilderingly) a crisp, blue, button-down business shirt. The idea is that you snuggle up in the crook of his arm and fall asleep. I mention this because I think it is funny, but am quite aware it hardly captures the spirit of this book – loving being *alone*, not getting comfort from an ersatz, one-armed, headless lover in a business shirt. Ho hum.

Of course I'd love my heart to catch and feel a shockwave run through me like a conga eel. Or meet someone as thoughtful and romantic as my English father, who placed a sheet of corrugated iron outside my parents' bedroom window so my Kiwi mother was reminded of the sound of home when it rained. And who wouldn't have wanted to be on the receiving end of Tom Fletcher's wedding speech (McFly – google it!). Several divorced women I know have found love, quite unexpectedly and very happily, with another woman (Elizabeth Gilbert included, apparently). Good for them.

I am now at a place where my happiness is not contingent on meeting someone. A relationship is optional; friendships are not. A man (or possibly a woman...) is the icing, not the cake. I cannot imagine compromising or relinquishing my independence. But everyone is different and for some, a mate is high on their list.

What do I want?

As I get older – and this is exacerbated the longer I live alone – I am less willing to compromise in any aspect of my life, and that includes dating. I have a fully functioning dickhead radar and am well aware that the length of my 'must have' list for a prospective beau is in inverse proportion to my chances of meeting him. Top of the list is a curious mind and wit, followed by a love of travel and walking in the rain, knowing what an okapi is, and how to make spaghetti Carbonara (no cream!), appreciating that supermarkets in other countries are as interesting as museums, having a penchant for spicy noodles, being solvent, knowing how to spell, or at the minimum knowing where to put an apostrophe. Or spell 'apostrophe' if it comes to that. Doesn't move his lips when he reads – that's a deal breaker. And being young enough not to be able to braid his nasal hair. Am I asking too much?

Parsley, peaches or pizza? Being realistic

The chances of meeting someone as you get older are much higher if you are a man than a woman. The Japanese have coined a word for this. Single women over 30 are called *paarsuri*, or parsley, because that is the only thing left on the plate. Depressing, huh? Even if I was brave enough to dip a toe in the dating pool, I don't care to be rejected.

--------------------------------- ✳ ---------------------------------

'Single is not a status. It is a word that best describes a person who is strong enough to live and enjoy life without depending on others.'

AUTHOR UNKNOWN

73

As Dita Von Teese said: 'You can be the ripest, juiciest peach in the world, and there's still going to be someone who hates peaches.'

At the moment I am happily adopting the *che sera sera* ('whatever will be will be') philosophy. But I am well aware that if and when I am ready to meet someone, they are not going to knock at my door as I sit in my navy-blue Lands' End nightie watching Netflix and eating diavola pizza. I know I will need to get out there and join that gym, do that evening class, volunteer for that thing, say yes to that invitation I'd rather decline, and so on. But you can only do so much. The best relationships are effortless and are born from friendship, which is why internet dating seems counterintuitive. But you can't argue with the numbers and a huge percentage of relationships start on line. The stigma about finding love this way has disappeared, but I fear my emotional skin is too thin and I haven't got enough patience or frog-kissing courage in me to take the plunge. I can't see myself swiping right any time soon. Right now I am happy living MOTH (Man Of The House) free.

✳

'It's better to be single with high standards than
in a relationship settling for less.'

AUTHOR UNKNOWN

Of course, there is always the possibility of meeting a stranger at an event you have an interest in – a concert, a talk, a foodie dinner or an evening class. Try accepting every single invitation for a month or two. My failures at connecting in these circumstances outweigh my successes, but you never know who you might meet. If you are out of practice making new connections, you could do worse than to take a leaf from Dale Carnegie's classic bestseller (30 million copies sold!) *How to Win Friends and Influence People.* In a nutshell, be interested in people, smile, remember their name ('the sweetest and most important sound in any language'), be a good listener, talk about their interests and make them feel important. Sounds like good advice.

Maybe I am a 'Quirkyalone', an interesting (if slightly mannered) term coined by journalist Sasha Cagan to identify people who are all for romance, but would rather be happily single than in a relationship just for the sake of it. In her book, *Quirkyalone: A Manifesto for Uncompromising Romantics,* she talks about 'the tyranny of coupledom' and I agree with her. Looking at couples from my side of the fence, that life sometimes seems oppressive. Maybe I'm growing more cynical, but the thought of someone saying 'you complete me' makes me shudder in a way I usually reserve for mime artists.

I am single, but somehow making a *thing* of it feels a wee bit 'the lady doth protest too much, methinks'. For example, wearing a 'single ring'… On a website selling these, they suggest 'My life is fabulous as it is, yet I am open to the possibilities'. The ring is 'an empowering reminder to the members that they are already complete'. Hmmm. I prefer the De Beers buy-yourself-a-right-hand-diamond-ring concept. ('The left hand says 'we', the right hand says 'me'.)

5.
YOUR
'VILLAGE'

I never made much of an effort to talk to strangers. I was always in a rush, running from work to the children and just 'being busy'. That has changed over the time I have been living alone. You learn to appreciate a smile or kind word from a neighbour, shop assistant or café owner. Sometimes it is just enough to quench a thirst for connection. It reminds me of the Sufi story about a man who says, 'Master, I've discovered the answer! Knock and the door will be open to you'. The master replies, 'Who said the door was closed?' When we feel alone, we still have an asteroid belt of different communities orbiting us. Family, friends and work colleagues are the closest, but don't dismiss the neighbourhood.

It might sound contrived, but I have set myself a challenge to make a new local friend by the end of the year. I have a dog park nearby, full of sociable neighbours, which is a good place to start. Here I have to confess that I recently entered Rory into the local dog show, where he won the fancy-dress class dressed in a home-made Sherlock Holmes outfit ('Sherlock Bones'). It was a one off, and I think might be God's way of telling me I had too much time on my hands. That said, I have arranged to have a glass of wine with the lovely woman who sponsored the show and who also happens to live alone, so there's my new local friend quota successfully met already!

In Australia about 40 per cent of us know our neighbours. It's not only nice to have someone know your name, but there will also be times when you need them – for something important (an accident, illness) or not so important, like moving a heavy piece of furniture.

On a more philosophical note, there is something about connecting to your broader community that evokes the spirit of 'Ubuntu', the South African belief in a universal bond of sharing that connects us all. There is no literal translation, but it means 'I am because we are.' The point is that you might be alone as you read this, but you are never really alone. You are part of humanity.

A final thought. Two legs or four?

People who don't live alone patronisingly assume that a pet can be a substitute for a human companion and a certain cure for loneliness. Wrong on both counts. I have a dog, and when he is away, the heart of the house seems empty. But that said, Rory is a *dog*. A pet. I love the fact that he welcomes me ecstatically, forces me to go for walks and occasionally actually smiles at me. But he is not a replacement for a two-legged friend. Nor is he my 'fur friend' or my 'fur child'. We don't have philosophical discussions about Nietzsche, watch *Game of Thrones*, or share dinner and a bottle of red. A companion, absolutely; a substitute for a human relationship, no.

✳

'You can't stay in your corner of the forest waiting for people to come to you. You have to go to them sometimes.'

AUTHOR UNKNOWN

TAKE AWAYS

Put yourself at the top
of the list and learn to
like who you are.

Make an effort with your family.

Look after your friends,
but don't be afraid to
weed and make new ones.

Move on from past relationships
and decide if you are ready
for romance.

Cultivate your 'village'.

Chapter 4

STAYING HEALTHY

Writing a personal health plan: mindset; nutrition;
physical and mental health ∗ *Losing weight*
∗ *Solo health issues and how to avoid them*

Your health is everything. You can't seize your days if you ignore your body. Living alone bumps health up to the very, very top of the soloist's priority list. The harsh reality is that there is no one at hand to help you if things start deteriorating or go badly wrong. You can, and should, make sure you have a veritable Greek chorus of health professionals behind you, including a Goldilocks of a GP (not too old, not too young, just right), whom you respect and trust, and a group of friends you can call on. But prevention is better than cure and you are your own safety net. Your friends aren't interested in your minor (or even major) health problems. You have to take responsibility for your health. If I ever find myself becoming complacent, I only need to remember the correlation between health and independence.

You are your own safety net

In *Living Solo*, Nancy Goldner talks of 'climbing the age ladder solo'. I'd rather be climbing it two steps at a time than hauling myself up the rungs like James Caan in *Misery*. Helen Gurley Brown called marriage 'insurance for the worst years of your life'. I don't have that insurance and am determined – have to be – to be as independent as possible for as long as possible. I want to ensure I get to do all the things I want to do, and that no one has to wipe my bottom until I'm good and ready. Actually, I never want anyone to have to wipe my bottom. I find that a mighty incentive. There is also a financial motive. Doctors and illness are expensive. Medicare data shows that 30 per cent of all the money you spend on healthcare will be spent in the last six months of your life.

You might have noticed that I bang on like a barn door about the importance of self-reliance. When it comes to health, self-reliance also means *taking back control and sovereignty of our bodies* in a world that is set up to help us fail, with transport (not feet) that moves us effortlessly from a to b, conveniently processed and packaged food, and entertainment that is spoon fed to our laptops.

This chapter will show you ways to call your own shots. It's in two parts: the first about writing a personal health plan; the second looking at how we can defy the accepted health implications of living alone. We're good at pushing back.

'The greatest wealth is health.'

VIRGIL

PART ONE:
A PERSONAL HEALTH PLAN

Take a cold, hard look at yourself, healthwise. To do this objectively, get a top to toe professional health check (either from your GP or a specialised private service). That will provide an empirical benchmark measurement and is the perfect point to confront yourself if you need to fix something.

Assess yourself honestly

Most of us take our health for granted like an old car, metaphorically spraying a coat of paint over it rather than looking under the bonnet and consciously poking about. To quote W.H. Auden, 'Death is the sound of distant thunder at a picnic'. For many years I managed to disassociate my actions and lifestyle from their impact on my body, but recently I have begun to feel a little out of kilter and disconnected to it. Not surprisingly, there came a time when my body said, 'If you don't give a damn about me, I won't give a damn about you'. Little things started to twinge, spasm, snap, dangle, leak, grow, flop or drop off. Our bodies are truly incredible machines, rigged with all sorts of early warning systems, such as changes in blood pressure, cholesterol levels, weight and BMI. Your body is constantly giving you messages. It is your job to listen.

I am tired of being tired. I ache not to ache. I want to feel what it feels like to feel great. I have been running with scissors for so long that I think I have forgotten. Feeling average is normal. I want to give my body the chance to see what it is capable of if I work with it, rather than against it.

Our bodies give us a second chance

Our bodies are amazing biological machines, not least because they possess an enormous, astonishing and persistent capacity to heal and repair. They are amazingly forgiving. (Just for starters, they produce two and a half million new red blood cells every second.) Human bodies are elastic bands, wanting to get back into shape. There comes a point when you can't go on borrowing against the future, but it is never, ever, too late to pick up healthy habits.

Writing my health plan

As an organised, systematic person, the idea of writing a health plan appealed. But not being a naturally svelte, kale-munching, Bikram-hot-yoga chick (more bison than gazelle), I had to come up with a plan that was realistic enough to (really, honestly, truly) integrate into my life. Something sustainable.

Simple things work, so there are only five parts to my plan:

1. Mindset
2. Nutrition
3. Physical health
4. Mental health
5. Facts and figures

✳

'In a disordered mind, as in a disordered body,
soundness of health is impossible.'

CICERO

Some people like to write a physical plan, while others are happy keeping the information in their heads. You will instinctively know what is right for you, *if you listen*. Naturally your plan will evolve and change over time, depending on what works.

1.
Mindset.
Head first,
then body

It's important to get your head into the right space as you approach your health strategy. Our brains are the most powerful organs in our bodies, and we need to harness that power. What do you think would help shift your mind towards embracing a healthier lifestyle and integrating it into a routine? What motivates you? What is holding you back, and how will you overcome the inevitable speed bumps? It's important to identify them, so you know what to do when the going gets tough. Which it has a habit of doing. Here are some things that have helped me.

Find images that motivate you It could be a picture of someone you admire (Brienne of Tarth!) or your 'before' photo as the wallpaper on your phone, or where you'd like to be in a year, or simply that beach you've always dreamt about.

Find a 'health mantra', or design your own:

- Fitness is 100 per cent mental. Your body won't go where your mind doesn't push it.
- Nothing is impossible. The word itself says *I'm possible.*
- You are entirely up to you. Make your body. Make your life. Make yourself.
- Every journey begins with a single step.
- No matter how slow you go, you are still lapping everyone who's sitting on the sofa.
- I am powerful.
- I am in control.
- Success does not come to you… you go to it.
- Energy flows where attention goes.
- Motivation gets you started; habit keeps you going.
- Make one healthy choice. Then another.
- Exercise to be fit, not skinny. Eat to nourish your body and always ignore the haters and doubters. You are worth more than you realise.
- Today is the chance to change yourself for the better. Simply do it.
- I'm working on myself, for myself, by myself.
- Note to self: 'I'm going to make you so proud.'

'The groundwork of all happiness is health.'

LEIGH HUNT

Small things make a difference This thought encourages me to dive in and make small changes, rather than waiting for The Right Moment, or for 1st January to roll around with the Resolutions Charade in tow. Be happy with a second loop around the park, or a green juice instead of a ham and cheese croissant. Both will nudge the ship in the right direction. Research has shown our bodies respond rapidly and appreciate the smallest of changes.

Enjoy the feeling of being in control Knowing that I have a plan for my health gives me a feeling of confidence. It also protects me from the unsolicited advice and criticism of well-meaning friends. (And isn't there a lot of it?)

Self-care How you approach your health, and its effect on your body, is a public reflection of how much you value and care for yourself. Or not. Take charge of your health; don't treat the doctor like a repair shop.

I don't *have* to do anything. I *choose* to do it Change your language. 'I *have* to go to the gym because...' or 'I *choose* to go to the gym because it makes me feel...' 'I *have* to avoid wheels of brie the size of my head because...' or 'I *choose* to eat this beautiful dewy bowl of berries because it makes me feel...' We are in control of what we do. No one is forcing us.

Most of my life I've lived in my brain. Now it's time to live in my body.

I will treat my body like a business Everything I do – work and pleasure – requires energy. Being unhealthy is a thief of productivity.

JFDI The world rewards doers. It's just about *doing* stuff. Planning, thinking and writing about your health is good; doing stuff is the bomb. Even a humble drop of water can erode a rock if it drips consistently. As Zig Ziglar said: 'Do it, and then you will be motivated to do it.'

2.
Nutrition

Heather Morgan had it right when she said: 'Every time you eat or drink you are either feeding disease or fighting it.'

Eating well is simple. If you came across a poor fish swimming unhappily in a tank of dirty water, you would clean the tank and change the water immediately. Do the same for yourself. Eating nutritious food is the single most powerful thing we can do to improve our health and fire up our body's powerful self-healing properties (even more than exercise). As my enviably lithe midlife friend Josie puts it, 'It's all about what you put into your mouth'. Food is by far the number one cause of preventable death and disease in the USA and where Americans go, we tend to follow.

It's an obscene fact that these days many more people will cark it from eating too much than not enough. Millions of years of healthy life are lost because of poor food choices. It's about so much more than the latest fad for 'clean' food. Fresh, whole, unprocessed, especially plant-based foods are repositories of *prana* or 'life energy'. Food with life force will give you energy. They say that if you eat food made by people in white coats then that's what you can expect in later life.

I am not going to patronise you by telling you specifically what to eat. You know the drill: eat more colours in your fruit and veggies than Joseph had in his dreamcoat (especially dark green leafy vegetables like silverbeet, cavolo nero, kale and spinach); protein (from lean meat, beans or lentils); wholegrains; good fats; nuts and seeds. And no added salt. The trick is to find recipes that you really like. Even if the only thing you do is stop eating crap, it will have a profound effect on your body. God knows, I have played artery roulette with abandon for years, but now feel the compulsion to stop. Good nutrition starts in the supermarket. Specifically, the outer rim of the supermarket. But then you know that too.

You also know your personal nutritional *bêtes noires* better than anyone. Too much sugar, take-away dinners, leftovers for breakfast, big portions or cosying up to the Wine Witch (a wonderful phrase coined by the Soberistas blog)? It's up to you to find replacements that fit the task. Build a file (physical or digital) of healthy recipes that you like, split into breakfast, lunch, dinner and snacks, so that you always have inspiration at hand. In my folder the breakfast section has juice and smoothie recipes (chop the fruit the night before and put in the blender in the fridge for the morning), plus savoury muffins and healthy

'When diet is wrong, medicine is of no use. When diet is correct, medicine is of no need.'

AYURVEDIC PROVERB

toppings for half a wholegrain English muffin. Avocado is a firm favourite at breakfast. Especially with Vegemite. (I know, I know!) Also, Greek yoghurt with berries and oats. Lunch is mostly vegetarian soups, salads and wraps. I'm going through a vegetable fritter phase for supper at the moment. Any vegetable that wanders into the kitchen is in danger of being grated, mixed with an egg, shallot, chilli, flour, herbs and spices and being pan fried in a spritz of oil. Delicious, crispy and healthy. Other regular suppers include a chickpea curry for one, or a baked sweet potato (start in the microwave, finish in the oven) with homemade (fat-free!) refried black beans, avocado and yoghurt. 'Snackcident' avoiders include roasted pumpkin seeds with sriracha and lime, crunchy oven-baked dukkah chickpeas and homemade microwaved popcorn with smoked paprika, or a banana with a little almond butter on it.

Of course, the magic combination is good food *plus* exercise.

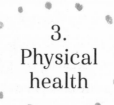

3.
Physical health

The truth bomb is that physical exercise isn't optional. Ouch. I try not to think of exercise as 'Exercise with a capital E' but just something we humans are designed to do naturally. Neanderthal women weren't waiting at home, sweeping the cave and knocking up brontosaurus burgers. They were out there hunting with the best of them. I'm afraid the clichéd 'use it or lose it' is true. In their book *Younger Next Year for Women* Chris Crowley and Henry S. Lodge cannot emphasise this point enough. 'If you don't send any signals to grow, decay will win, but even a modest signal to grow – a decent workout, even a good, stiff walk – will drown out the noise. Thing is, you need to tell your body it's springtime.' So I try not to over-think exercise and just get on with it.

The best advice is that the ideal form of exercise is the one that you'll actually do. So for me that rules out running, mountain biking, surfing and ballroom dancing (but never say never). At least we have more choices than ever before of finding something we enjoy. Living alone gives you the time and opportunity to cast your net wide when it comes to trying new things. There are usually one-off trial classes available so if you make a fool of yourself, you know you are not committed and don't have to ever go again. Become a scientist of your own exercise experiments and check how you feel after each one.

I prefer to exercise alone. Walking is my daily exercise. I try to do 10,000 steps a day (easier now there is a pedometer on my phone). I do enjoy it, but it can become a bit monotonous, so here are some suggestions to boost its impact:

- Switch on your core as you set out, pull your tummy button towards your spine. Be aware of your pelvic floor.
- Time your walk and try and beat it.
- Every five minutes do some step ups or run for 60 seconds.
- Make a special walking soundtrack: two slower tracks alternating with each fast one.
- Walk on different surfaces – sand, grass, footpath.
- Run up and down every set of stairs you come across on the walk.
- Make sure you are on a flat, even surface, then walk backwards for a bit, to exercise underused muscles and help balance.

I also dip a toe into the gym, do easy yoga (via YouTube) and boxing to a DVD at home. I like going at my own pace in my own time. I have a yoga mat and a couple of weights: a teeny weeny home gym! The fact is that (as 'The Clothesline Diet' elegantly proved) you don't need equipment. The internet is a marvellous resource for workouts and motivation. Search around YouTube to find the type and intensity of workout you're after and, more importantly, an instructor you like. Try Daily Burn or Body Groove for starters.

Don't forget core and pelvic floor exercises. We (women!) have 10 orifices. Seven above the waist and three below. If you don't want the lower three leaking in later life, get squeezing! I put little stickers on my steering wheel, fridge, handbag and wallet to remind me to do pelvic floor exercises. I'll never be able to rival the infamous Patpong Thai ladies with the ping pong balls, but I'm OK with that.

If you need a bit of motivation to exercise, here are some thoughts.

- You always feel better after exercise. Always. It *gives* you energy rather than depleting it. Write down or just acknowledge how you feel after exercise. I find this good motivation as I have never, ever, regretted it.

- Don't think too far ahead. Just take it one day (or workout) at a time.

'A bear, however hard he tries, grows tubby without exercise.'

A.A. MILNE

- Remind yourself why are you exercising in the first place. Imagine the way you want to look or feel. Have your goal/goal weight on Post-it notes everywhere. My goals are strength and suppleness.
- Go shopping! Buy some comfortable, practical, attractive gym gear (I like Lands' End online) and proper shoes. Chuck out all those old horrors.
- Have your exercise gear ready to step into first thing in the morning, or your gym bag packed and ready to go.
- Every bit of exercise adds time to your life, and we all want to increase our allotted number of spins around the sun, don't we?
- Each workout empowers you more than the last one. It's a process of multiples – the more you do, the more you can do. It's incredibly satisfying when you find a workout routine getting easier.
- Enjoy the feeling of being in control and not having anyone else patronise you because you are not as fit as they are.
- Make a schedule, put it in your diary and stick to it. Find the time of day that suits you best and incorporate it into your routine.
- Do a Steve Jobs on it. He always wore a black turtleneck, jeans and sneakers so he had one fewer decision to make every day. So reduce decisions by making yourself a timetable, with a different exercise for each day. Monday yoga. Tuesday walking and so on.
- Weigh in weekly and fill it in on a chart. There are plenty on line, but I prefer graph paper. Fill it in with ink, not pencil!
- Make a commitment contract with yourself (with a penalty clause). Keep a workout log – up the ante with yourself and focus on your progress.
- Reward yourself when you've completed a mini goal: a book, a magazine, a facial, a massage, a mani-pedi.

- Tie a little friendship bracelet or cotton string around your wrist as a touchstone to remind you why you're doing this.
- Give yourself a seven, 10, 30, 60, or 90 day challenge.
- Be as physically active as possible throughout the day.
- Some people, even (especially!) some of your friends, will want you to fail. You know it's true. Do not let them win. Success is the best form of revenge.
- Change the way you perceive yourself, from 'a non-exerciser' to 'someone who is physically active'. Be your own before and after case study.
- Make a fitness vision board on Pinterest.
- Think about the next time you have sex. You want to be confident. (And fit!)
- Get enough sleep; you know what is optimal for you. We all have two cords running through our lives: one pulls us to get up and get going, while the other draws us back to be still and replenish. Find the right balance. Don't get so exhausted you can't even finish a sen

'It is exercise alone that supports the spirits and keeps the mind in vigour.'

CICERO

4.
Mental health

Like an onion, or a cross-section of the earth with its molten centre, we are multi-layered beings. At the core is our mind – our nerve centre, literally and metaphorically. Mental health is about the way we think and feel and how capable we are of dealing with life's inevitable ups and downs. It's about the storm inside. Nurture yourself from the inside out, mentally first, then physically.

Mental health is just as important as physical health, and the onus is on those of us who live alone to self-monitor. We have to notice changes in our temperament and be honest with ourselves. For example, identifying feelings of lack of self-worth that lead to overeating and calling ourselves out on it, or watching ourselves mask aching loneliness with bluster and bravado or alcohol.

Of course you must reach out for professional help if you need it, but in the spirit of self-reliance we need to learn to look after our own mental health. The UK's Mental Health Foundation suggests the following 10 practical steps to take care of yourself mentally:

- Talk about your feelings
- Eat well
- Keep in touch
- Take a break
- Accept who you are
- Keep active

- Drink sensibly
- Ask for help
- Do something you're good at
- Care for others

Another aspect of mental health is mental agility. I live in terror of finding myself in a retirement home singing the first verse of 'Nelly the Elephant' over and over again. While there is no guarantee that won't happen anyway, keeping your mind nimble can reduce the odds. Here are some tips from Harvard Medical School:

<u>Keep learning</u> This includes doing a job that keeps you mentally active, or learning a new skill or hobby.

<u>Use all your senses</u> If you engage all of them as you learn, more of your brain will be used to retain the memory.

<u>Believe in yourself</u> If you believe you can improve your mind then you have a better chance of keeping it sharp.

<u>Prioritise brain use</u> Keep yourself as organised as possible to leave room for new and important information.

<u>Repeat what you want to know</u> Either out loud or write it down.

<u>Space it out</u> Repetition works best when it is spaced out (the opposite of cramming for an exam), so re-study after an hour, then every few hours, then every day.

---

*

'Our bodies are our gardens, to the which our wills are gardeners.'
WILLIAM SHAKESPEARE, *OTHELLO*

5.
Facts and figures

Prepare a file where you collate your statistics, including weight, cholesterol levels, blood group and pressure, BMI and any other numbers that are relevant to you, such as test results and details of your parents' health records. Date the page, so that you can use it as a benchmark. Schedule in any tests you are due to have (Pap smear, optician, dentist, dermatologist etc) and see your GP to clear up any little niggly things that have been bothering you. Do it.

Losing weight: The elephant in the room

Excess weight is the first worldliest of first world problems. Sadly, food loves me every bit as much as I love it, and I have paid the porcine penalty. Being overweight is draining and it makes life harder than it needs to be. Weight is often an issue for people living alone and it is my personal Achilles heel. I am very much a work in progress. Did you know that baby sperm whales can put on 90 kilograms in a day? I know, because I did it on holiday in Italy last year. I'd rather not suffer the fate of Queen Victoria, who grew so big they had to cut a hole in her bedroom floor and lower her down on pulleys when she died. She got buried in a square coffin. We know that many Australians are digging their graves with their teeth and that the Standard Australian Diet is just that – SAD.

One of the wonderful things about living alone is that it is a No Judgement Zone, so you can watch the trashiest of reality TV with gay abandon, knowing there's no one sitting there, lips pursed. The bad thing about the No Judgement Zone is that there's no one watching as you dive into a bag of chips the size of Nevada or gorge on a piece of cheese that's rich and powerful enough to invade a country. If it's not in the house then you can't eat it (or drink it, for that matter).

I was definitely thinner when I was married, and whenever I did lose weight I enjoyed basking in His Approval. It is much harder when you are by yourself and you have to be your own cheer squad. I know there are a million ways to lose weight and some of my friend have had great success (including with the CSIRO, Weight Watchers and 5:2 diets). From cabbage soup, Atkins, South Beach, Mediterranean, Forks over Knives, Dukan and Du-kan't diets, the fact is they all work *if you follow them*. After a lifetime of trial and error, I have come to the obvious conclusion that the only way to lose weight is to figure out what works for *me personally* and then do it.

I have resigned myself to the fact that I'll never be as slender as a piccolo, but am trying to get to a weight where my body and clothes are comfortable, and I feel good moving through space. I could do a PhD on losing weight and know that it starts with believing you deserve better. As Dr Phil said: 'If you begin to require more of yourself, that in and of itself is different.'

'Health is a relationship between you and your body.'
TERRI GUILLEMETS

Here are a few things that have worked for me:

- Opinions differ, but when I am trying to lose weight I keep it private.
- Make up a mantra to say to yourself whenever you need it. Mine is: 'It's just about one choice at a time.'
- If I'm going to a restaurant, I look up the menu online beforehand so I can work out the best food options.
- I try to drink the equivalent of the Hoover dam every day. To make this easier, I bought a citrus zinger water bottle that has a juicer at one end. Money well spent. I drink water before every meal.
- I try new foods every week. (Hello vegetable spaghetti, hello shirataki noodles, hello daikon, hello dragon fruit.)
- If you are about to eat something derailing, brush your teeth.
- Cut down on meat (think of it as a flavouring, not the main event).
- Cutting down on alcohol is a huge one. A bottle of wine has the same calories as a Big Mac. Some friends have given up completely (like Clare Pooley, author of the witty and brave *Sober Diaries*) and I haven't ruled that out completely, but I am trying to stop drinking alone, or just have one glass with supper. I have a tiny carafe that I decant wine into and limit myself to that. And I've switched to small glasses: it makes a difference. The same with small plates.
- I have my repertoire of go-to healthy 'temple food' recipes in one file, divided up into different meals. I try to stick to three meals a day plus two snacks, and sometimes track what I eat.
- I let myself have one meal a week (usually on Friday night) when I feast on whatever I want. It's strange – you'd think I'd want to eat a bowl of spag bol the size of small car, but somehow I don't.

- I use a body brush before a shower. It gets the blood flowing and makes me more aware of, and connected to, my body.
- Try chewing gum instead of snacking.
- If I'm really tempted, I just go to bed with calorie-free Netflix.
- If you slip up, get back in the mindset and start again. Miles Davis said that if you hit a wrong note, not to worry. It's the next one that makes it good or bad.

THE SUPER SIX: feet, forks, fingers, sleep, stress, love

This is Dr David Katz's summary of the advice he gave to a patient to tip the health odds in their favour.

<u>Feet</u> Physical activity is linked to weight control, reduced inflammation, enhanced immune function and reduced cancer risk.

<u>Forks</u> A nutritious diet has wide-ranging effects on every part of the body and lowers the risk of chronic disease.

<u>Fingers</u> This one is about holding a cigarette. Don't. If you tick the right answers in these first three boxes, you reduce the risk of chronic disease by a staggering *80 per cent*.

<u>Sleep</u> The quality and quantity of your sleep has a profound impact on your body and mind.

<u>Stress</u> Known as 'the silent killer', stress must be managed to avoid long-term impact on your health. It seems quite bizarre that some people wear sleep-deprivation as a badge of honour ('I'm so stressed').

<u>Love</u> Clinical studies have shown that people with loving relationships are less vulnerable to chronic disease.

PART TWO: SOLO HEALTH ISSUES AND HOW TO AVOID THEM

When I started investigating the health implications of living alone, I was dismayed by the quantity of research that appears to demonstrate its adverse health effects. While I don't question its veracity, none of us wants to be a statistic and we soloists are a contrary bunch, more than capable of proving the research was an anomaly. Here are my thoughts on how we can say '*uck the research'!

*uck the research #1 STAY CONNECTED

Loneliness kills. That's the conclusion of a study by Brigham Young University researchers, who claim to be sounding the alarm on what could be the next big public-health issue, on a par with obesity and substance abuse. According to their research, the subjective feeling of loneliness increases risk of death by 26 per cent.

Confronting stuff. This report consists of a comprehensive review of more than 70 health studies over 35 years, with more than three million participants. 'Social isolation' and 'living alone' were found to be more harmful to health than 'feelings of loneliness', increasing mortality risk by 29 and 32 per cent respectively. This is the same level as the increased risk of death from obesity.

✳

'The more you eat, the less flavour;
the less you eat, the more flavour.'

CHINESE PROVERB

These figures might be depressing, but they aren't exactly new. Previous research by Dr Holt-Lunstad and Timothy Smith showed that isolation and loneliness threaten longevity as much as smoking 15 cigarettes a day or being an alcoholic. They surmised that this could be because isolated people are less likely to see a doctor 'and also maybe have poorer health habits, like smoking, drinking and lack of exercise'.

How incredibly patronising! They conclude that it is important not only to maintain meaningful close relationships but also a 'diverse set of social connections'. Duh.

*uck their research by:

- Making relationships a priority (and not just the close ones, but embrace a wide circle of friends and acquaintances).
- Staying active and engaged.
- Being truthful and tough on yourself when it comes to your own health.

✳

'Friends are like walls. Sometimes you lean on them and sometimes it's good just knowing they're there.'

AUTHOR UNKNOWN

*uck the research #2 YOU DON'T NEED TO BE MARRIED TO BEAT THE ODDS

Further research shows that if you have cancer, being married can bring greater benefits than chemotherapy, adding fuel to the staying healthy/ living alone fire. Researchers from Harvard University followed 750,000 patients and found that married sufferers had a 20 per cent better chance of survival all round, and that for breast and colon cancer in particular, the benefits of marriage outweighed the benefits of chemo.

Before you log on to RSVP, or start watching episodes of *Say Yes to the Dress*, let's have a look at what it is about being married that goes towards ensuring better outcomes, and how we can knit that into our solo lives.

*uck their research from a practical perspective:

- Observation. If you are around someone all the time, you notice even subtle changes in their behaviour and their body. Make sure your best friends are alert to this. Arrange to have regular check ups, whether you feel you need them or not.
- The nag factor. A partner will nag and nag until you make the appointment to have something checked out. We have to nag ourselves.
- Have a support team. Build a network of people you can rely on.
- It is less stressful financially with someone to share the burden. In the absence of that, get on top of your financial situation immediately (see Chapter 6). Having financial control and autonomy is critical. Unfortunately, private health insurance discriminates against single people and single premiums can sometimes cost the same as for a couple, so shop around carefully.

*uck their research from an emotional perspective:

- Without motivation to impress the person you live with, you have to love and impress yourself.

- Having someone to exercise with is definitely an incentive. That's what friends, gyms and trainers are for.

- Download in the evening – get a journal, record a video diary or call or Skype a friend.

- Feel loved, wanted and noticed. Stay connected and look after your relationships: tell family and friends how much they mean to you and, likely as not, it will be reflected back. Arrange regular catch-ups.

- Be appreciated for what you do for others. It will be noticed and when you need help yourself, it will be there.

*uck the research #3
LIVING ALONE DOES NOT MEAN YOU WILL BE DEPRESSED

A Finnish report showed that living alone increased the risk of depression by up to 80 per cent. 'Living alone may be considered a mental health risk factor,' said lead author Laura Pulkki-Råback PhD. Just because there may be more of a likelihood of people living alone being brushed by the wings of depression, one does not automatically lead to the other. Hold on to that thought. Depression is a common and highly treatable condition. Monitor yourself to check that loneliness doesn't morph into debilitating depression. Research by the University of Queensland found that when people suffering from depression joined a social group that meant something to them, they reduced their risk of depressive relapse by 24 per cent. If they joined three groups, their depression dropped by 63 per cent. Dr Tegan Cruwys, who ran the study, said, 'If you think about some of the key symptoms of depression, it's also about a loss of purpose in life and feeling alienated. These are the things that groups directly target. They give you meaning, they give you a reason to get out of bed in the morning. They tell you there's a place for you in the world and they make you feel as though you're part of something bigger.' Can't argue with that.

Julie Holland MD is a psychiatrist who wrote the book *Moody Bitches: The Truth About the Drugs You're Taking, the Sleep You're Missing, the Sex You're Not Having, and What's Really Making You Crazy.* While very supportive of prescription drugs for acute mental conditions, she believes we are generally over-medicated. 'I do believe that too many women are being told to medicate away their essential, authentic selves.' It's food for thought: sometimes it is good to feel really strong emotions and weather the storms. I am not making light of depression, but peaks and troughs are part of life and you can become a more powerful and resilient person by battling through them. Seeing a counsellor, as well as or instead of medication, can give you tools to help long term, rather than just masking the symptoms.

---- ✳ ----

'Our body is a machine for living. It is organised for that, it is its nature. Let life go on in it unhindered and let it defend itself, it will do more than if you paralyse it by encumbering it with remedies.'

LEO TOLSTOY

Nothing boosts your mood like having a sense of purpose and I hope this book encourages you to think about that. According to Dan Buettner's *The Blue Zones: Lessons for living longer from the people who've lived the longest*, people who have a sense of purpose live seven years longer than those who don't. Don't worry if your Sense of Purpose eludes you just now. Be patient. Simply working towards small and simple goals will enhance your mood. And while we're on the subject of Blue Zones, try their True Vitality Test, which gives you a likely life expectancy, plus another older age you can expect to reach if you make some changes. Mine went from 87 to 100!

 ✳

'When I am taking my last breath, I want to look at how I used up the best of myself. How much did I sweat, push, pull, rip, fall, hit, crash, explode? My dream is to be so well-used that in my last half second, I will burst into dust.'

ELIZABETH STREB, *HOW TO BECOME AN EXTREME ACTION HERO*

TAKE AWAYS

Accept responsibility for
your health. You are
your own safety net.

Get regular health checks,
whether you feel
you need them or not.

Write a personal health plan,
incorporating mindset, nutrition,
physical health, mental health
and facts and figures.

Don't accept the research
findings about the health of people
living alone: stay connected,
watch yourself, use common sense
and reach out if you need to.

Chapter 5

COOKING FOR ONE

Why it's worth it ✳ *Overcoming obstacles*
and outsmarting the system ✳ *Ingredients,*
equipment and bulletproof recipes for one

Cooking for one isn't easy. Most of us can come up with a long list of excuses for why it's all too hard.

<u>Excuse #1</u>: 'I can't be bothered.'
<u>Excuse #2</u>: 'Supermarkets cater for families.'
<u>Excuse #3</u>: 'Every recipe in the world serves four.'
<u>Excuse #4</u>: 'It's easier to eat unhealthily than healthily.'
<u>Excuse #5</u>: 'I've run out of ideas.'

But I think I've cracked the code. It does involve another mindset shift, a bit of trial and error and some shopping. (Hurrah!)

Instead of thinking of it as a chore, approach cooking for yourself as an opportunity to find your culinary voice and try new ingredients and recipes when the stakes aren't high. What's the worst that can happen?

After much trial and error I have found dishes for one that work beautifully: Singapore noodles, stuffed chicken thighs, fresh Vietnamese spring rolls, baby corn and noodle fritters, miso lamb chops and linguine with clams. I'll share all these recipes later.

You can cook anything you like. No compromising. And you never have to eat anything you don't like, ever again. I'd rather lick an electrical socket than eat tuna, and guess what? I don't have to. Nor do I have to cater to anyone else's whims, food intolerances or predilections: wheat, nuts, seeds, sodium, dairy, soy, eggs, fish, shellfish, sesame, Natterjack toads and carbs after 5 o'clock (bring 'em on) are all welcome in my kitchen.

By the end of this chapter I hope to have equipped you with inspiration, practical advice and a few recipes you'll want to try. They are just suggestions: I am not an instruction barker; I am an offerer of ideas. Now let's do away with those excuses.

Excuse #1: 'I can't be bothered.'

Pottering in the kitchen, listening to a podcast or watching a gnarly Swedish detective series on my laptop, glass of wine in hand, chopping, stirring, tasting, washing up as I go and then eating at my little square kitchen table (complete with tablecloth and candle) is my absolute favourite end to the day. It is a present to myself. Sometimes I have to force myself to accept invitations out, I love it so much. I always have to evaluate: 'Is it better than an evening cooking by myself with wine and Netflix?'

With no one else to please, consider, nourish, satisfy, seduce, cater for or impress, the goalposts shift. 'It's not worth cooking just for myself' is a phrase I hear over and over again. Cooking isn't everyone's cup of tea, and there are times when cheese on toast hits the spot, but I'm not letting you off that lightly. It is a bit like the chicken and the egg because, as Delia Smith says, 'It *is* worth the bother, but until you bother, you won't discover the satisfaction'. More from Delia (Patron Saint of Solo Cooks) later.

Of course it is worth it, because you *are worth it.* (A L'Oreal moment.) Just as it's worth buying flowers to put by your bed, or sleeping on good sheets, or lighting a candle at dinner, or going to an art exhibition alone. Cooking is not just about the end result (fresh, delicious, nutritious food that makes your taste buds do the samba); it is an important component of self-care and an opportunity to find your voice. Experiment until you find a collection of dishes that you love.

Excuse #2: 'Supermarkets cater for families.'

Yes, they do. The cards are stacked against the solo cook and we have to work around the system. Supermarkets are complicit and don't attempt to cater for us, although we number in the millions. The chance of bagging a bargain at Costco, where the food is cheap but is packaged for

---

*

'I once read cooking is something you do for your family. But when you're alone you sometimes have to treat yourself like family. And now that my apartment's redolent with the smell of food it feels more like a home than a box where I hang my hat.'

WAITER RANT

Walton-sized families, is remote. Three-fers, two-fers and BOGOFs ('three for the price of two', 'two for the price of one' and 'buy one get one free') don't float my solo boat. And don't get me started on the loyalty card schemes that are based on a minimum spend per week. When will the supermarkets wake up?

Keep an eye out for the sections of the store that support a single cook. Like the meat or deli counter, where you can buy a single chicken breast and a couple of slices of cheese or ham. (This is easy if you are lucky enough to have a local butcher or fishmonger.) The bulk bins (also in health food stores) are good for buying small amounts of nuts and seeds, and salad bars are useful when you only need one or two stalks of celery, not a bunch the size of a palm tree. I only buy as much fruit and veg as I know I can eat in a day or two, as they are usually the first things (along with bags of soggy salad) to be thrown out. A shocking one-third of all of the food we buy is thrown away. I have to shop more often, but that's my 'normal' now.

✳

'Preserve and treat food as you would your body,
remembering that in time food will be your body.'

BENJAMIN WARD RICHARDSON

The freezer section is good for baby peas, spinach (frozen in little blocks), raw prawns, mango and berries for smoothies, puff pastry and authentic Italian wood-fired pizza bases. I refuse to buy individual frozen meals. But I freeze my own leftovers in containers or plastic bags.

Mother Nature, bless her, has designed plenty of food for one: most fruit, along with eggs, corn on the cob, sweet potato, baby eggplants, field mushrooms, a bunch of asparagus, fish, an artichoke, a small lobster, a lamb shank, a single chicken breast or thigh, and a steak, for starters. French shallots are great mini substitutes for onions, and Brussels sprouts for cabbage. Mini cans of corn and mixed beans are useful discoveries. Marigold Swiss Vegetable Bouillon Powder is a pantry favourite of mine (and of a certain Nigella!) – it has no added colourings, flavourings or preservatives and is available from health stores. I buy the large drum and use it in everything from pasta sauce to stir-fries and soups that need stock. With its light, clean, natural taste it's also good as a hot non-caffeinated drink.

And you don't have to rely on the supermarket. If you live in a city, visit the less familiar neighbourhoods, or take a 'food safari' tour. Explore a variety of ethnic food stores and discover a world of wonders. I keep a basket of Asian sauces next to the cook top. A starter kit includes dark and light soy sauces, rice wine, rice wine vinegar, black Chinkiang vinegar, fish sauce, mirin and Shaoxing wine, with oyster sauce, white miso, hoisin, chilli bean paste and red curry paste in the fridge. In the freezer I have pancakes for Peking duck, kaffir lime and curry leaves, edamame (soy) beans and Malaysian roti bread (which is fantastic dry-fried when it puffs up dramatically, and is perfect for mopping up curries).

Excuse #3: 'Every recipe in the world serves four'

As well as equipping me with a touch of eccentricity, a noisy sewing machine and a childhood of regularly replaced Start-Rite shoes (I shudder to think how many times my feet were x-rayed in the Clarks Pedoscope), my mother gave me a copy of Delia Smith's excellent *One is Fun!* cookbook. The exclamation mark lends a whiff of desperation, but it was the first book to recognise that people living alone deserved attention and that dividing recipes by four or eating leftovers night after night wasn't going to cut it. Delia understood that not all recipes can be scaled down (quarter of an egg anyone?) and that cooking times and temperatures need to be adjusted for smaller quantities.

Beyond that, I think she was very perceptive and prescient in her introduction: 'One of the subtlest but, I suspect, most pervasive problems in modern society is that (often carefully hidden) lack of self-acceptance, and I really believe that a conscious effort to care for ourselves – especially when eating, which we do two or three times a day – is a most marvellous antidote to this. Eating (and cooking) an interesting, satisfying meal does make, I am certain, a great contribution to our feeling of well-being.' Well said, Delia.

While researching this chapter I trawled the internet and bought every cookbook for one I could lay my hands on. The results were disappointing. Most of the books, blogs, websites and links are flawed for one reason or another. In some, all the recipes serve two or four people (go figure...) or list ingredients such as 'one anchovy fillet', 'quarter of a small onion', 'one tablespoon sour cream', 'two fresh rice noodle rolls' or 'a quarter of a tin of tomatoes'. Is it just me, or is this barmy? (And don't get me started on *Microwave Cooking for One*. Yes, it's a real book. No, don't buy it.) Accessible, delicious, workable recipes for one are as rare as silver-horned unicorns. Do not despair; all is not lost.

Ironically, the best cookbook for one by a country mile is *The Complete Cooking for Two Cookbook* (I know, I know) by America's Test Kitchen. I'm a fan of their *Cook's Illustrated* magazine. They are self-professed food nerds, working in a vast kitchen in America, where they test and re-test recipes, tweaking an ingredient here or an oven temperature there, to produce recipes that are guaranteed to work. Their book is a winner.

The Complete Cooking for Two Cookbook is huge, with 650 recipes covering everything from the basics (shopping, storing, leftovers, kitchen essentials) through to soups, salads, meat and vegetarian dishes, breads, cakes and the rest. There are lots of good things about this book. Every recipe starts with an enlightening 'Why this recipe works' paragraph, there are tips and tricks dotted throughout, recipes are handily tagged 'light' or 'fast' and there are even lists of emergency substitutions and '10 things you didn't know you could freeze'. Yes, you still have to divide the recipes in half, but they have done the hard yards for you method-wise. Some of the best recipes include the grill-smoked

'So many of the pleasures of life are illusory,
but a good dinner is a reality.'

JOSEPH CHAMBERLAIN

pork chop, parmesan-crusted asparagus, vegetable and bean tostadas and lasagne baked in a meatloaf dish.

Joe Yonan's two books, *Serve Yourself: Nightly Adventures in Cooking for One* and *Eat Your Vegetables,* get an honourable mention, partly because Joe seems to be the only writer of solo cookbooks who was *actually living alone* when he wrote them! They are Southwestern in flavour and some of the ingredients are not familiar or available to us, but I love his enthusiasm and easy breezy style of writing. Some of my favourite recipes include chickpea, spinach, feta and pepita tacos, fusilli with corn sauce and curried butternut squash risotto.

Both Joe and Delia have a system where they cook a double batch of a simple base and then make two entirely different dishes. Delia calls them 'mixed doubles'. Fried minced beef and onions make cheese and herb crusted cottage pie one day and spaghetti with Mexican sauce the next. Joe's spicy black bean soup base becomes black bean soup with seared scallops and green salsa or black bean tortilla soup with shrimp. Risotto has a second life as dry-fried risotto cakes. Pop some cheese (baby bocconcini are perfect) in the middle for a gooey centre.

Things change so rapidly on the internet that I am wary of giving websites, but at the time of writing, the best solo cooking blogs are

---- ✳ ----

'Tell me what you eat and I'll tell you who you are.'

JEAN ANTHELME BRILLAT-SAVARIN

Single Fare (a bit impersonal, but it does what it says on the tin), Singly Scrumptious, Cooking for One in Paris and 1–2 Simple Cooking. For general inspiration I also like the blog with attitude, Lady and Pups (check out the stained glass noodle recipe), Sorted Food, Closet Cooking, feedfeed and Taste. Pinterest and YouTube weren't much use at coming up with recipes for one. (Unless you want to watch scary vintage footage of Saint Delia going off piste and frying – yes, *frying* – a pizza for one.)

A few of my favourite recipes appear later in this chapter. Once you've found ones you like, keep them together in a file (digital or paper) and make them into a little book as a very welcome gift for another solo cook.

Excuse #4: 'It's easier to eat unhealthily than healthily.'

Pesto and pasta. My downfall in three words. I could happily dive naked into a pool of the stuff and eat my way out. An Olympic-sized pool. Eating healthily is one of the easiest and one of the hardest things to do by yourself, and you know why. Easy because you don't have to take anyone else's tastes into account and you are in complete control of what comes into your home and goes into your mouth. If you don't buy that family-sized box of Maltesers then it's not going walk from the supermarket onto your sofa, is it? But it's hard because no one is watching you. So if no one sees you eating leftover mac and cheese for breakfast, did it really happen? Like the butterfly that flaps its wings in the Amazon, I'd love it if my slip-ups went unnoticed but for me it's true that 'What you eat in private you wear in public'.

To encourage myself to eat healthily this is what I do:

- I try to visualise the effect of the food I'm eating on my body. You know how you feel your very cells singing when you drink a fresh juice? I try to picture nutritious food cleaning my body from the inside out.
- I ask, 'Is it *nurturing*?'
- Lifeless food gives you lifeless energy. Imagine a table groaning with yellow–brown food – chips, fried foods, hamburgers, biscuits, packaged bread and pizzas. Now imagine a table holding a rainbow of fresh fruits and vegetables, so brimming with vitality that you can see them breathing. Both tables give you energy in the form of calories, but only one will give you vitality and 'energy' in its true sense. It's the same feeling you get in the fruit and vegetable section of the supermarket compared to the meat section. While I am not planning to become vegetarian or vegan, I do find myself drawn more and more to these recipes.
- Imagine writing down what you eat for a week, then giving it anonymously to someone to describe the sort of person you are. What would they say?
- Scour the internet, go to the library for cookbooks and magazines to develop a repertoire of healthy recipes that you enjoy, so you won't feel you are compromising. Some good healthy food sites include Anna Jones, Naturally Ella, Minimalist Baker, Food Heaven Made Easy and 101 Cookbooks.
- Clean your fridge thoroughly; you'll be surprised how dirty it gets. And, while you're at it, throw away anything out of date or unhealthy. If it's not in the house you can't eat it.
- I always keep a bag of baby spinach in the fridge. Chopped up, it

can be added to anything and 'disappears' while adding lots of nutrition. (Blocks of frozen spinach do the same thing.) So I chuck handfuls into pasta sauce, casseroles, stir-fries and soups a couple of minutes before serving – the vitamin fairy has visited.

- Plan meals in advance and write down everything you eat.
- Fall in love with soups and smoothies.
- Make your water quota more interesting by flavouring it with mint, strawberries, watermelon, grapes, lemons or limes.
- Use spray oil and a non-stick pan for frying. It's amazing how little oil you actually need.
- Alter ego time. Would the person I want to be eat this?
- Remember Michael Pollan's succinct advice: 'Eat food. Not too much. Mostly plants.'

Excuse #5: 'I've run out of ideas.'

I'd be the first to say there's nothing wrong with eating your favourite dishes over and over again. More bowls of chilli con carne and spag bol have passed my lips than I care to remember. However, there comes a point when you know it's time to go exploring and get back your

'The aroma of good chili should generate
rapture akin to a lover's kiss.'

ORIGINAL 1951 MOTTO OF THE CHILI APPRECIATION SOCIETY INTERNATIONAL cooking mojo. Treat it as an adventure and an opportunity to expand your palate and repertoire. Why not pick a particular cuisine – Japanese, Thai, Lebanese, Mexican – or a more obscure one – Persian, Laotian, Peruvian – or vegan – and make yourself an authentic expert? Right now I'm working on perfecting my xiao long bao dumpling technique.

Get different cookbooks from the library or ferret around second-hand stores for gems. (I'm transfixed by my latest bargain, *Graceland's Table: Recipes and Meal Memories Fit for the King of Rock and Roll*, featuring 'Love Me Chicken Tenders' and 'Blue Suede Berry Pie'. But I digress.) To shake things up a bit, try different ways of eating – drinking soup from a cup and saucer, using chopsticks, or eating cold Zaru soba noodles and dipping sauce from a bamboo mat set in the special serving tray you can buy in Asian shops.

Equip yourself

Although these aren't specifically designed for solo cooks, my can't-live-without pieces of kitchen equipment are:

- Global vegetable knife 15 cm/6 inch (good for everything)
- Silicone spoon-shaped spatula (the ultimate bowl/pan scraper – I use mine every single day)

'One cannot think well, sleep well, love well, if one has not dined well.'

VIRGINIA WOOLF

- Non-stick ovenproof 20 cm/8 inch frying pan. Fries with hardly any oil and is also good for oven-baked risotto
- Bendable Ikea plastic chopping boards. Fold the board and tip the chopped ingredients straight into your saucepan and peelings into the bin. You'll be converted – use a green one for veggies and a red one for meat
- Spanish water glasses – I love Bormioli Rocco Bodega Maxi Glass 510 ml tumblers. They are a great shape – big and thin – and I try to hoof down a whole glass every time I walk past the kitchen sink. Another way to reach your daily water goal
- Wooden pepper mill
- Wooden spoons – I have two huge pots of spoons on the kitchen counter. I love the feel of them and use them for everything
- Inexpensive blue and white Chinese bowls – small rice bowls for side salads and cooking ingredients; larger ones for noodles, soups and as serving bowls
- Silicone and fabric double oven gloves
- Graters – both the traditional box and a microplane, which delivers snowy clouds of Parmesan over roasted vegetables and pasta
- A mandolin to make wafer thin salads from cabbage, fennel and the like...

I keep my eyes peeled for small-sized kitchen equipment that might work especially well for one. Cooking and serving food in mini individual dishes make your meal feel more special and controls portion size. Some favourites include a 340 g/12 oz mini oval stoneware cocotte (casserole), perfect for baking a stuffed chicken thigh or a mini potato gratin; little stackable bamboo steamers (for four dumplings or a piece of fish); a Vietnamese clay pot; a mini meatloaf tin; a white French porcelain lion's head soup bowl and some small white enamel pie dishes. I've kept a couple of teeny jam pots from plane meals and serve myself mustard or sambal in them.

Consider a good counter-top toaster oven as an economical and speedy alternative to your conventional oven. It is *the* perfectly designed piece of equipment for the solo cook. It can roast a small chicken or bake a tray of vegetables and most can grill as well.

A dishwasher can take a week to fill up when you are alone, but I still wouldn't go without mine and, as I rinse the dishes before they go in, it doesn't smell. You can get slimline and compact dishwashers but, guess what? They cost the same as a regular dishwashers. Sigh.

Quick tips for the solo cook

- When freezing a chicken breast, thighs or lamb shank, add some olive oil, garlic and fresh rosemary or a soy sauce/ginger/garlic/chilli mix into a zip plastic bag before you freeze for magical marinating while it thaws.
- Use clothes pegs to close bags of flour, sugar, cereal, pasta, rice, salad etc.
- When cooking pasta, save time by boiling the kettle for the water.
- Use baking paper (or 'inbetween paper') to separate rashers of bacon, chicken thighs etc when freezing so that you can easily remove just one.
- When freezing soups or sauces such as bolognese or chilli, put them in zip plastic bags, push out the air, label them and freeze them flat. Most efficient use of freezer space!

- Every veggie is improved by roasting! Not just potatoes and pumpkins – try asparagus (sliced in two, north–south), cauliflower, broccoli, zucchini (courgettes), tomatoes or Brussels sprouts. Toss them in a splash of olive oil and add your favourite spice. Try cumin and smoked paprika, or just salt and pepper. Or make zucchini ribbons with a vegetable peeler and grill on a ridged pan with a spritz of oil for a lovely zebra snack.
- Grate ginger and garlic on a cheese grater.
- Keep a list of what's in the freezer, to help you use things up.
- Experiment with a new ingredient every couple of weeks (I've done guava, farro, daikon, Sichuan pepper, pomello, rambutan and spaghetti squash) or give an old favourite, such as rockmelon, parsnip, fennel, artichoke, beetroot, mussels or star anise a guest spot back in the repertoire.

———————————— ✳ ————————————

'Oh! The pleasure of eating my dinner alone!'

CHARLES LAMB

Meals for one that don't need a recipe

The simplest meals are usually the best. I shared a wonderful dinner in Tuscany with my mother years ago. We ate a perfectly ripe fig draped in wafer thin prosciutto, followed by one perfect sausage, a little roasted potato and plain green salad, then a white nectarine. Perfection. The style guru Sir Terence Conran once moaned about airline food, asking why they couldn't just serve fresh baguette, gooey brie and a green apple? Simple, but perfect. Like Elizabeth David's omelette and a glass of wine, or Antonio Carluccio's motto 'mof mof' (minimum of fuss, maximum of flavour). To pull off meals like these you need quality ingredients, but even reaching into your pantry and frying up garlic and chilli flakes in good olive oil, adding some cooked pasta and sprinkling with parsley and parmesan can be pure *aglio e olio* store-cupboard heaven.

Here are some ideas – they aren't really recipes, more suggestions. They are all forgiving, so you can substitute or wing it with abandon. And who doesn't love a recipe you can describe in a few sentences?

'Enchant, stay beautiful and graceful, but do this, eat well. Bring the same consideration to the preparation of your food as you devote to your appearance. Let your dinner be a poem, like your dress.'

CHARLES PIERRE MONSELET

CHEAT'S QUESADILLA

Keep burrito wraps in the freezer. Microwave a couple back to life then make a sandwich with grated cheese, sliced chilli, rocket, spinach, salami or ham – whatever you have lurking in the fridge. Microwave for about 30 seconds to start melting the cheese, then put in a heated non-stick frying pan (no oil) and cook on both sides until golden. Cut into triangles like a pizza. So delicious, so quick, and great if someone pops in unexpectedly.

A DECADENT CHEESE FONDUE FOR ONE

Unwrap a baby Camembert and put it back in its wooden box with the lid on the bottom, if it came in one, or in a small earthenware bowl if it didn't. Cut a small garlic clove into 6 or 8 pieces and jab them into the cheese rind, along with a few rosemary sprigs. Bake in a 180°C (350°F) oven for 15 minutes, then split the rind with a knife and dip bread in. Eat the rind too.

A QUICK SALAD DRESSING

This will have you eating mountains of the green stuff. A splash of soy sauce, rice wine vinegar, mirin, a drop of sesame oil and a squeeze of lime (and a bit of miso paste if you want) all whisked together. Or a teaspoonful of miso paste mixed into mayonnaise. Delicious over a simple salad of finely sliced cabbage, spring onions, mint and toasted flaked almonds.

HOT GREENS

Heat a couple of tablespoons of good olive oil, fry a chopped garlic clove and throw in a handful of greens – cavolo nero, silverbeet, kale or spinach – until wilted, then pour on the juice of half a lemon and a handful of grated parmesan.

KALE CHIPS

Wash, dry and cut up kale. Spread on an oven tray and spray with olive oil, then add some chilli flakes and lemon and put in a hot oven for 15 minutes or until crispy.

OVEN PARCELS

En papillote (French for 'in parchment') means the food is put into folded baking paper or aluminium foil and baked. You can put anything inside, from a chicken breast (slice it in two lengthways so that it's not too thick) or a piece of fish along with sliced vegetables, herbs, a splash of wine or stock, olive oil or butter, salt and pepper. Fold up the parcel carefully (Bon Appetit have a good video that shows you how) and bake at 180°C (350°F) for about 25 minutes. Impressive, special, healthy and versatile. A little present to yourself!

SIMPLE VEGETABLE SOUP

Spray a pan with oil. Grate a small onion and a garlic clove and cook until translucent. Add chunks of whatever vegetable you fancy – a chopped up head of broccoli (including the middle of the stalk) or half a small head of cauliflower or some pumpkin. Add a potato if you want it creamy. (For extra flavour, roast the veg first, sprayed with oil and some s&p.) Add enough veg stock (I use water and the Marigold brand bouillon) to cover, add some pepper and any herbs you have and boil for about 10 minutes until the veg is cooked. Cool a little and then liquidise. Taste for seasoning. Sometimes I cook a little pearl barley separately and add it in, or add a small can of mixed beans if I want it a bit heartier. Finish with cubes of cheese or a snow cloud of microplaned parmesan.

ZUCCHINI (COURGETTE) SLICE

Grate a large zucchini, mix with half a cup of self-raising flour, half a cup of extra tasty cheddar, salt and pepper and 1 or 2 beaten eggs (depending on the wetness – it should be a bit runny). Pour into a small baking tin lined with baking paper, sprinkle with a little more cheddar and a little paprika and bake at 180°C (350°F) for 30 minutes. Delicious hot or cold and freezes beautifully.

QUICK BAKED SPUDS

Prong a potato or two (sweet or normal) and microwave for 5-10 minutes, then pop in the oven for about 30 minutes at 180°C (350°F) until the skins are crisp. Pour some healthy homemade soup, such as broccoli or pumpkin, over the top as a low-fat sauce (recipe above). Or, if you can be bothered, scoop out the inside, mash with some butter, grated cheese, soy sauce and cumin, spoon back into the skins and grill, for the most more-ish twice-baked potatoes.

QUICK CHICKPEA CURRY

Grate an onion and a garlic clove and fry until translucent. Stir in a tablespoon of curry powder or paste and cook until fragrant. Add a tin of tomatoes, simmer for 15 minutes, and add a tin of drained chickpeas and cook for 5 minutes more. Throw in a handful of chopped baby spinach or couple of cubes of frozen spinach for extra vitamins and a dose of self-righteousness!

SAVOURY PANCAKES

Mix together 100 g (3½ oz) plain flour, 1 egg, 125 ml (4 fl oz) milk and a pinch of salt. Make pancakes and stuff with cheese, spinach and ham or whatever is in your fridge.

SIMPLE BEANS

Fry an onion and a clove or two of garlic, then add a tin of beans (such as cannellini) and their liquid and cook for 20 minutes – or drain them and add a tin of tomatoes and boil for 10 minutes. Finish off with basil and a flick of parmesan. Quick and delicious.

PARMESAN BISCUITS

Perfect to take over to someone's house or good to nibble with drinks if someone's coming by. Grate a handful of parmesan (or Grana Padano, which is just as good) and chop in some walnuts and fresh rosemary. Put into little piles on a baking tray lined with baking paper and bake at 160°C (320°F) oven for 5 minutes, watching like a hawk, because one minute they're underdone and the next minute they're burnt! Remove from the oven when golden, leave to cool a bit, then put them on a wire rack to cool down completely.

Breakfast ideas

I try to mimic the enticing breakfast buffets at deluxe hotels by cutting up and arranging fruit the night before so it's ready first thing in the morning. The same with any fruit and veg you might want for smoothies/juices. Put it in the blender the night before – if it's convenient, you'll eat it.

I retired the huge fruit bowl in favour of a smaller one, which holds one or two day's worth of fruit. This might be a couple of mini bananas, an apple, a passionfruit and a punnet of blueberries, all washed and ready to go. I have a little plastic 'breakfast basket' in the fridge, which has non-fat or Greek yoghurt, oats, granola, chopped almonds and mini plastic boxes of LSA and flax seeds with a spoon in them. With the contents of my little breakfast tray, plus bags of frozen berries and mango, I can always make a healthy breakfast (including smoothies) with zero effort.

For a simple cut-fruit salad, chop the fruit really small – apple, pear, banana, date, melon, mango, berries etc – so that you get loads of different tastes and textures in each mouthful. Serve with yoghurt and muesli.

As an alternative savoury brekkie, I also have individually frozen slices of grainy bread or wholegrain English muffins, ready to be

———————————— ✳ ————————————

'Life, within doors, has few pleasanter prospects than a neatly arranged and well-provisioned breakfast table.'

NATHANIEL HAWTHORNE

toasted, and I spread them with a quarter of an avocado, a spritz of lime and a bit of sambal oelek. Delicious. (If you keep the stone in the avocado, spritz it with lime or lemon juice if you have some, wrap it tightly in plastic wrap and whack it in the fridge; it lasts fine.) You can add some low-fat ricotta and sliced tomato or maybe a snowy dusting of finely grated parmesan for a change.

Or how about a bacon sandwich for a treat? I take low-fat bacon out of the pack and separate slices with 'inbetween' paper and freeze them. No need to defrost – with just a quick whiz in a non-stick frying pan I can have just 1 or 2 slices with some avocado or tomato on half a wholegrain English muffin on a weekend morning. It really is quite modest, calorie-wise. Another good alternative is a savoury muffin – perhaps tomato, basil and ricotta – using a frittata type recipe. I make batches of six and they sit happily in the freezer until I either take one out the night before or zap it in the morning.

Lunch

Chomping through samey samey sandwiches or slurping your way through bowl after bowl of soup can get a wee bit monotonous. So I try to create a bit of lunchtime variety with different textures. Maybe a bento box or a ploughman's lunch, consisting of some crumbly as-sharp-as-they-make-it-Cheddar, wholegrain crackers, slices of green apple, some radishes, a teeny pot of sambal, a slice of prosciutto and some roasted almonds or pepitas. A grown up lunch box!

Another favourite lunch is just a bag of salad, poured into a bowl, and then I search through the fridge to see what will pep it up. Maybe a few slices of dry-fried haloumi or chorizo sprinkled with lemon or balsamic (avoid balsamic glaze, the work of the devil).

Ring the changes with some fresh Vietnamese rice paper rolls. These are a delicious, low-fat option and having the dried wrappers in the cupboard makes them very convenient (they keep indefinitely). Dip a couple of the stiff wrappers in warm water then lay them on paper towel to dry. Pour boiling water over a small amount of rice vermicelli noodles and rinse well. Then assemble a bit of avocado, grated carrot, a slice of cooked chicken, some rice noodles, shredded lettuce and any fresh herbs you have (mint and basil work well) on the wrapper – whatever you want really, just don't put in too much or you won't be able to roll it properly. Add a bit of sweet chilli sauce or hoisin, make sure the filling is in the centre of the wrap, then fold in both sides and roll tightly from top to bottom. If you lay the mint leaves (or half sliced prawns) on the wrap first you can see them through the skin and they look very pretty. You can make an easy dipping sauce by mixing 2 tablespoons of hoisin with 1 tablespoon of peanut butter. If this sounds complicated, it's not! There are lots of tutorials on YouTube and once you've tasted them, you'll be hooked.

I think it's worth splurging on really beautiful freshly baked bread once in a while. It's perfect for sandwiches the first few days, then it's toast time, or toasted cheese sandwiches, and finally we're in breadcrumb and crouton territory. It's still worth it, just for that taste on day one.

'Luncheon: as much food as one's hand can hold.'
SAMUEL JOHNSON, *A DICTIONARY OF THE ENGLISH LANGUAGE*, 1755

The better you store it, the longer it will stay fresh – the best way to do that is to keep it in a brown paper bag, then wrap a tea towel around it and just keep it on the kitchen counter. Of course, bread also freezes really well.

While we're on the subject of toasted cheese sandwiches, look up Jamie Oliver's 'Number 1 Toasted Cheese Sandwich' – it will blow you away. It even has a cheese crown. I feel my arteries hardening just typing the words.

Dinner ideas

The 80:20 rule applies to my recipes as well as to my wardrobe – I use the same 20 per cent of recipes 80 per cent of the time. Here are some of my favourites that you can use as a 'jumping off point' and experiment to your taste.

ONE STORE-BOUGHT BARBECUED CHICKEN = FIVE MAIN MEALS

Day 1: Chicken and oven-roasted vegetables

Carve off a breast and serve with roasted vegetables and giant Israeli couscous – fry a chopped French shallot, put the couscous into the pan to toast a bit, then add stock and simmer for 10 minutes until done. Toss in some chopped baby spinach.

Day 2: Burritos

Shred some leg and thigh meat and add to a warmed burrito with avocado and a mini tin of mixed beans. Top with grated cheese and shredded lettuce.

Day 3: Vietnamese Chicken Salad

Shred the other breast and make a Vietnamese salad with shredded cabbage, spring onions and mint. Pick the remaining meat off the bones and put in the fridge. Make stock using the bones – cover the carcass with water in a large pan and add an onion, a couple of celery stalks, a chopped up carrot and a few peppercorns. Simmer for an hour or two on low heat (otherwise it will evaporate). Strain, let it cool and then put in the fridge.

Day 4: Dumpling Soup

Skim the fat off the refrigerated stock and heat half of it in a pan. Make dumplings with the leftover chicken, a spring onion, some ginger and garlic – whatever you have really – fold up in wonton wrappers and cook in the hot broth for about 5 minutes. Sprinkle with shredded spring onion.

Day 5: Risotto

Heat the remainder of the stock with a pinch of saffron in a small saucepan. In a frying pan, melt a tablespoon of butter and a little olive oil and cook a small chopped onion or French shallot until soft. Add half a cup of arborio rice and fry until translucent. Add a quarter cupful of dry white wine and stir until it is absorbed. Gradually stir in the hot stock, bit by bit, until the rice is the right texture – about 20 minutes of stirring and adding. Add some Parmesan cheese and serve with a green salad.

SINGAPORE NOODLES
(ADAPTED FROM *ONE IS FUN!* BY DELIA SMITH)

Boil the kettle. Place 1 heaped dessertspoon dried shrimp and 3 dried Chinese mushrooms in a bowl, cover with boiling water and soak for about 30 minutes. Drain, keeping the mushroom water, then chop the mushrooms into small shreds, discarding the hard stalks. Soak 75 g (2½ oz) rice noodles in a bowl of boiling water for a few minutes and then drain. (Don't oversoak, or they will fall apart when you stir-fry.)

Meanwhile, heat up 2 tablespoons oil in a frying pan and, while that's heating, assemble together on a plate the shredded mushroom, dried shrimps, 1 chopped onion, 2 chopped bacon rashers, 1 chopped garlic clove and 1 tablespoon grated ginger. When the oil is hot, throw them all in, stir well, then reduce the heat to very low and let the ingredients cook gently for about 15 minutes (this slow cooking allows all the delicious flavours to permeate the oil).

Then add 1 teaspoon Madras curry powder. Turn the heat up to medium, add some shredded breast of a cooked roast chicken and 25 g (1 oz) fresh or frozen peeled prawns, followed by the mushroom water and the 4 finely chopped spring onions.

Add the noodles to the pan and toss well. Finally add 2 tablespoons soy sauce and 2 tablespoons sherry or Shaoxing rice wine, toss again and serve with a green salad.

'I cook with wine, sometimes I even add it to the food.'

W.C. FIELDS

HEALTHY SWEET POTATO SKINS

Preheat the oven to 200°C (400°F). Prick 1 sweet potato in several places. Microwave for 7 minutes on kitchen towel, then put in the oven on baking paper for 30–40 minutes.

Dry-fry 1 drained mini tin of corn in a frying pan with some Mexican chilli seasoning. Don't keep stirring it; let it roast and get browned. Mix it with 1 drained tin of black beans. Separately, fry a small onion or French shallot in a little butter or olive oil until translucent and add to the bean mixture.

Scoop out the flesh of the spud, mash and mix with 2 tablespoons cream cheese, 3 tablespoons Greek yoghurt, a couple of chipotle peppers from a tin with adobo sauce (or a dash of Tabasco), pepper and salt. Add the bean mixture and some chopped coriander. Put into the skins, add a bit of grated cheddar on top and grill for about 5 minutes until brown.

Alternative fillings:

Fry a chopped French shallot in a little butter, add a couple of handfuls of baby spinach and a tin of chickpeas. Mash the sweet potato flesh with cream cheese and Greek yoghurt, stir in the onion, spinach and chickpea mixture. Add s&p. Pop back in the skins and grill with cheese on top.

If you're in the mood for a little meat, fry a chopped onion or shallot, add 100 g (3½ oz) lamb mince, 1 chopped red chilli and a pinch of cumin (or 1 teaspoon miso) and cook until golden brown. Mix with the potato flesh, adding salt and pepper and a bit of mint if you have it.

If you want to, you can spray the skins with a little oil while they're 'empty' and put back in the oven for 5 minutes if you like them crispy.

(NB You can bake more than one potato and keep them wrapped up in the fridge for up to a week. Reheat in the microwave or a gentle oven.)

VIETNAMESE CLAY POT CHICKEN AND RICE

You can buy lovely, small, rustic, Vietnamese clay cooking pots with lids from your nearest Chinatown or on Amazon. The first time you use one, you need to soak it beforehand for 24 hours and use a low heat for the first 5 minutes. Dice 1 or 2 chicken thighs and marinate them in a dessertspoon of cornflour mixed with 1 tablespoon soy sauce, 1 tablespoon Shaoxing rice wine and a splash of sesame oil for about 30 minutes. Rehydrate a couple of dried Chinese mushrooms. Heat a tablespoon oil in a frying pan or wok; add 1 finely chopped garlic clove and a dessertspoon of minced ginger (you can use a cheese grater for both of these). Cook for 1 minute until fragrant, then stir in the chicken. When it starts to brown, add the chopped mushrooms, 70 g (2½ oz) rice, 1 tablespoon soy sauce and a dash of sesame oil. Keep stirring for a couple of minutes and then transfer the contents to your clay pot. Add 3 tablespoons of water and put over low heat for 5 minutes, then increase it slightly to medium. Check the pot every 10 minutes or so, and add more water if necessary. It should take about 30–40 minutes total, but about 10 minutes before the end of cooking you can add some chopped leafy greens, such as bok choy, or just stir in chopped baby spinach after you take it off the heat. Check for seasoning, put it on a trivet and enjoy!

TANDOORI CHICKEN

I happily cheat and use a good-quality bought tandoori paste here. I've made it from scratch and it's no better! (Same with beef rendang and Malaysian curry pastes.) Mix 1 tablespoon of paste with plain yoghurt (a ratio of about 1:6 depending how strong you like the taste) and squeeze in half a lemon. Either use 2 skinless chicken thigh fillets or 1 skinless breast fillet. If using thighs, remove any fat and small pieces of bone and whack with a meat hammer until thin, and slash the surface a bit. If using a breast, cut it in half lengthways, beat with a meat hammer and slash. Then marinate in the fridge for 1 hour or overnight. Take out of the fridge 10 minutes before you are going to cook and preheat the grill. Grill the chicken until it is cooked through. Serve with plain steamed rice and a green salad or in wraps with lettuce, yoghurt and mint. Keep leftovers and use in wraps, salads and sandwiches.

MISO LAMB CHOPS

Umami lick-your-fingers chops. This marinade also works miracles on pork, chicken and fish. Mix 1 tablespoon white miso with 1 tablespoon soy and 1 tablespoon mirin, spread over your lamb cutlets, marinate and then grill. (Adapted from *Lighten up* by Jill Dupleix.)

CHAR SIU PORK PANCAKES

Like duck pancakes, but made with pork. Get a small piece of pork fillet from the butcher – about 10–15 cm (4-6 inches) long. Marinate it in 1 tablespoon hoisin, 1 tablespoon honey, 1 tablespoon soy sauce, half a teaspoon sesame oil and a pinch of five-spice powder. Cover and refrigerate for a couple of hours or overnight. Halve a small Lebanese cucumber lengthways and remove the seeds; cut into matchsticks. Do the same with a spring onion, then chill them both while you cook the pork. Heat the oven to 200°C (400°F). Place the pork on a rack over a small pan half-filled with water (this will stop it from drying out). Cook for about 15–20 minutes, basting with the marinade a couple of times. Towards the end, brush with honey and pop under the grill briefly to brown. Remove and let it rest for a few minutes. Meanwhile, steam some frozen (Peking duck style) pancakes (available from Asian supermarkets). To serve, spread a little hoisin onto a pancake, add a matchstick or two of spring onion and cucumber and a slice of pork and roll up. Delicious, easy and special. Goes well with a plain green salad. (Actually, everything goes well with a plain green salad.)

TERIYAKI CHICKEN

I regularly make a double portion of this to use in rice paper rolls, or I wrap sushi rice around chopped-up pieces to make a non-seaweed sushi. Put equal measures (maybe quarter of a cup) each of soy, sake and mirin into a little saucepan and simmer for 5 minutes. Allow to cool, then marinate 4 flattened chicken thigh fillets in the sauce (or 2 breasts cut in half lengthways, then flattened). Grill or fry until golden. Great with steamed rice and salad. Sometimes I serve this for myself in a bento box, with salad, rice and a beautiful chopped-up chilled orange afterwards, all neatly arranged in the compartments.

STUFFED CHICKEN THIGHS

These are delicious and can be eaten hot or cold, which is why I usually cook four thighs at a time – two for dinner and two for leftovers. Flatten and trim 4 thigh fillets. Mix up a small quantity of sage and onion stuffing from a packet with boiling water, allow to cool, then place in a sausage shape along the centre of each thigh. Roll them up and then wrap bacon around each one. Pop on a small oven tray lined with baking paper and put in the oven for 40 minutes at 180°C (350°F), or until they are golden brown all over, turning them halfway through. The title doesn't really do it justice!

LAMB SHANK AND BEAN MASH

A bear hug of a dish. Lightly drizzle a lamb shank with olive oil, slip a sprig of rosemary and a couple of garlic cloves in their skin underneath and roast in the oven at 180°C (350°F) for 40 minutes. Remove the rosemary and slip the garlic out of its skin. Drain the worst of the fat away, then rinse and mash a can of cannellini beans (or butter beans) into the garlicky oil. Serve with the lamb and a crisp green salad.

BABY CORN AND NOODLE FRITTERS (ADAPTED FROM TASTE.COM.AU)

Since I got my new non-stick frying pans (which require almost no oil for frying) I have become obsessed with vegetable fritters. Soak about 40 g (1½ oz) dried rice noodles in boiling water for 3 minutes until softened. Drain and cut up with kitchen scissors. Combine 2 chopped spring onions, a packet of baby corn cut into small slices, 1 chopped long red chilli, 2 tablespoons soy, 1 tablespoon oyster sauce and a dash of sesame oil. Add a scant quarter cup of self-raising flour and 2 beaten eggs (if it needs to be wetter, add another). Pour a small amount of oil into a frying pan and fry spoonfuls of the mixture. Drain on kitchen towel. These are best just out of the pan, but extras will keep happily in the fridge and are nice cold, or just reheated in a dry frying pan.

Fritters are a great way to use any leftovers – chop up leftover roast meat and veggies, just add a couple of eggs and flour and fry them up.

LINGUINE WITH CLAMS

This recipe is from Nigella Lawson's *How to Eat*, which has an excellent chapter on cooking for one and two. This is an absolute favourite, worth making just to hear the clatter of the clam shells. Nigella writes so beautifully, but here, for the sake of brevity, I have paraphrased. Soak 200 g (7 oz) little clams (vongole) in cold water (to get rid of any sand). Cook 150 g (5 oz) linguine in boiling salted water. Undercook it slightly as you'll finish it off in the frying pan with the clam juices. Mince 1 clove of garlic. Gently fry it in 1 tablespoon of olive oil and crumble in half a dried red chilli. Drain the clams, throwing away any that are open, and add to the pan. Pour in a glass of white wine and clamp a lid on. In 2 minutes the clams should open up. Add the drained pasta and swirl about some more. Chuck out any clams that have failed to open. Add a tablespoon of parsley to the pan and shake about, then dish up, sprinkled with another tablespoon of parsley. Nigella finishes the recipe by saying: 'Cheese is not grated over any pasta with fish in it in Italy, and the rule holds good. You need add nothing. It is perfect already.' Absolutely.

One final story on this subject. Lucullus was a politician and renowned gastronome in ancient Rome. One evening his steward, hearing that he was not having company for dinner, served him a pretty average meal. Lucullus told him off, saying: 'It is precisely when I am alone that you are required to pay special attention to the dinner. At such times you must remember, Lucullus dines with Lucullus.'

Lucullus knew his worth and you should too.

TAKE AWAYS

Find your voice. Try new
ingredients and recipes - there is
nothing to lose. I can't be bothered.
Pah! Of course it's worth it because
you are worth it. Cooking is an
important element of self-care.

Outfox the supermarket bosses
and make it work for you. Explore
ethnic supermarkets.

Visualise how health food nourishes
you and gives you energy in
every sense. Review the tips and
incorporate the ones that
work for you.

Search out great recipes for one
and keep them in a file. I've listed
over 40 suggestions for solo meals.
Try one tonight - I dare you.

Chapter 6

SOLO FINANCES

The importance of money when you live alone
* *Writing a Financial Blueprint* * *Budgeting/saving/investing*

This is no time to be asleep at the wheel. Being on top of your finances is important to everyone, but when you live alone it must go to the very top of your priority list. I cannot overstate how crucial it is. You are not just self-reliant but also self-funded. Friends and relations can provide an emotional safety net, but when it comes to cold hard cash, you alone are responsible. The fact is that most of us, harsh though it is, cannot rely on anyone else to take care of us financially now, or in the future, and that includes your relatives, your children and the government.

But it's OK. Build your own safety net in the shape of a Financial Blueprint and you'll be on track. If you feel you're already in a good place financially, you can skim this chapter. But you'd be in the minority (and look, your nose is growing longer). Statistics show that most women are not in control of their finances and being alone makes that a particularly perilous position to be in.

The singles penalty

First, the bad news. We pay a premium for living alone. But you already knew it, didn't you? You don't have to be Einstein to work out that with no one to share the bills, a larger percentage of our income goes towards living expenses, even though many of them are the same as a couple or family or whole hippy commune would pay. Rates, insurance, water, electricity, gas, Netflix, internet and car expenses are virtually identical. We can and do pay huge premiums when it comes to booking holidays, hotel rooms or rental cars. It is a bitter pill to swallow, but the financial odds are squarely stacked against us.

The statistics make for sober reading. (The figures with an asterisk are from the US. The percentages in Australia and the UK may be slightly different, but the trends are the same.)

- 47 per cent of women over 50 are single and 50 per cent of marriages end in divorce.*
- In the first year after a divorce, a woman's standard of living drops by 73 per cent on average.*
- Of the elderly living in poverty, three out of four are women, yet 80 per cent of these women were not poor when their husbands were alive.*
- 90 per cent of all women will be solely responsible for their financial well-being within their lifetime.*
- Only 12 per cent of women think their superannuation will be enough for retirement. (Source: Financial Literacy Foundation 2008)
- Half of all women don't know how much they'll need for a comfortable retirement (Source: Financial Literacy Foundation 2008)

- The average woman retires with half the super balance of the average man. (Source: ASFA 2011)
- Life expectancy for women is currently 84, but it is going up, and you need to factor that in. (Source ABS)
- 40 per cent of all retired single women live below the poverty line. (Source: Industry Super Australia)

I know, the numbers are depressing but use them as a powerful incentive *not* to become a statistic. You need to be in control of your money, never the other way round. Dealing with finances is the final frontier of independence. This chapter outlines some clear steps to get you there.

I get it: I didn't want to think about money either

Before I wrote this chapter, I reorganised my cutlery drawer, did my tax return, mended a hole in a cardigan, cleaned the filter on the air conditioner, washed the dog and put a vase on eBay. You get the picture. Displacement activities I think those are called. Putting it off, in other words. Finances are not my great passion, but I do recognise that they are so important I have to turn towards, not away from, the monetary nitty gritty. Now that I am on top of it, I am happy to share the good news that it (like some of life's other great pleasures) isn't complex, doesn't take too long and gives you an immense feeling of satisfaction when you're done.

The principles of money management for those of us who live alone are exactly the same as for everyone else. (Why wouldn't they be?) It is just a case (once again) of *putting them into practice*. Tedious but true, it is like exercise or a diet – it only works if you make a concerted effort, so put it in your diary and take action. Sigh. I really don't want to sound like a bully, but I also don't want you to find yourself disempowered, having left it too late, drowning in financial quicksand, with no Lassie on hand to save you. Woof.

If you are worried about any one of these things…

- How much money you have
- Paying off your credit card in full every month
- Funding retirement
- Your ability to pay an emergency expense
- Not being able to afford a holiday
- Not saving enough money
- Bills
- Debt
- Never being able to treat yourself

… then you need to make a Financial Blueprint.

YOUR FINANCIAL BLUEPRINT

This 12-step Financial Blueprint is like an economic GPS: there to guide you. However, it is not actually about the money as much as it is about *you*. The Blueprint is divided into two parts:

The first part is about <u>how you think</u>:
How you treat money is a reflection of you
What is important to you?
How do you feel about money?
Adjust your mindset

The second part is about <u>what you do</u>:
Educate yourself
Budgeting
How long will your money last?
Be smart with your money
Saving and investing
Build a team
Essential documents
Taking action

'Never spend your money before you have it.'
THOMAS JEFFERSON

1. How you treat money is a reflection of you

'... how we treat our money speaks volumes about how we perceive and value ourselves. If we aren't powerful with money, we aren't powerful. What is at stake here is not money – it's far bigger. This is about your sense of who you are and what you deserve. Lasting net worth only comes when you have a healthy and strong sense of self-worth.' Brilliantly said, Suze Orman.

That is so insightful, and rings so true. Your money is an extension of you, so how you think, act and feel about your money is a reflection of how you perceive and value yourself. It starts with self-worth.

The most financially successful business people, from unknowns to Warren Buffett and Richard Branson, all share that sense of self-worth and confidence, and confidence begets confidence. It reflects.

2. What is important to you?

Money matters because it determines the options open to you and lessens the gap between where you are now and where you want to be. I hate being told what to do (and don't like fixed degustation menus in restaurants for that precise reason!) and I want to live life my way. That's what financial independence gives you.

Before we get into the numbers part of the Blueprint, articulate what is important to you, so that you know what you're aiming for. Answer the following questions. (There are no right or wrong answers. The point of the exercise is to define the role money plays in your life.)

- Picture the life you want to lead. How do you want to feel? How do you see yourself? Where will you live? How would others describe the way you live, having spent time with you?

- What's important to you? Seeing your family or children regularly, feeling secure, passionately pursuing your interests or exploring the world? All of the above?
- What personal goals would you like to achieve this year, and over the next five years? How do you plan to achieve them?
- Have you got any secret ambitions that no one knows about and that people would be quite surprised to discover? What do you need to help you get there? What's the time frame?
- How do you define financial security? Is it not worrying about bills, treating yourself without having to justify it, not having to work, knowing exactly how much you have and that it will last as long as you do?

3. How do you feel about money?

It's important to be clear about how you perceive money, as it informs our feelings and it is feelings that spur us to action. What associations does money have for you? Pleasure, fear, jealousy, worry, guilt, freedom, anxiety, ambivalence, joy? Does it bring people together or tear them apart? Or maybe you just don't want to think about it at all. Interestingly, the psychologist Valerie Wilson found that the four words most commonly associated with money are all negative. They are: anxiety, depression, anger and helplessness.

'The real measure of wealth is how much you'd be worth
if you lost all your money.'

AUTHOR UNKNOWN

Our parents and upbringing can profoundly influence our attitudes towards money. These perceptions can be quite hard wired, but it doesn't mean you have to behave in the same way. In my family, anything to do with money was my father's domain and it was considered impolite to discuss it. When I got married it was a model I subconsciously adopted and my (now ex) husband looked after our joint finances. I find it amazing, looking back, how willing I was to relinquish that power. When my father died I had to unravel a labyrinth of knotty financial affairs of which I had no knowledge. When my marriage ended I had to trust others to report on our financial status because I didn't know, and I realise now that the seeds of my divorce were sown in that ignorance. Never again! I know to the cent exactly how much I have, and where it is.

However you feel about money, acknowledge it and use it as an indicator to help define how you will approach your financial situation.

4. Adjust your mindset

Many women feel powerless when it comes to money. Shake that vulnerability off your wings. It's important that you approach your Blueprint in the right frame of mind: ambitious, confident and striding big Usain Bolt steps towards happiness. Be strong and think big.

'When I was young I thought that money was the most important thing in life; now that I am old I know that it is.'

OSCAR WILDE

These might help you along the way. Pick and choose the ones that resonate.

- Increase your revenue. Work for as long as you can, doing anything that you can. It not only provides income and gives you the ability to borrow money to invest, but also gives you self-respect, makes you feel valued, engaged and useful and keeps your brain sharp. Don't talk yourself down at work. You can earn more. Agree your KPIs in your job and smash them, enabling you to ask for a salary rise. Try and freelance at something you're good at. Jump in!

- Being financially independent gives me an insulating layer of security. Security makes me confident and confidence makes me happy.

- I control my money, not the other way round.

- I decide what to do with my money – I know I can make myself powerful with my money.

- Money directly affects my future happiness, so I need to understand it better than anyone else. I can ask for help, but I need to be the one pulling the strings.

- Being proactive is the way to go.

- It is never too late to start. Taking action is the way to kill fear.

- I think of myself as my own company: The Jane Company Ltd. I am the CEO and CFO of the company, and I am responsible for the P&L, investment strategy etc.

5. Educate yourself

One of the best ways to increase your confidence about money is to learn more about personal finance. No one will ever care about your money as much as you do, so it's important that you are comfortable with the language and principles involved. At the most basic level, there is nothing more to it than primary school arithmetic and some new vocabulary. If you feel you already have a good grasp, push yourself with more complex strategies. Do not be afraid to ask questions. (Remember when we were at school and the good teachers knew that the only 'bad question' was one that hadn't been asked?)

There is so much good, free information available. There are more books, seminars, websites, podcasts and YouTube videos about personal finance than you can shake an abacus at, and it won't take long to find one that you like. My favourite is the bestselling *The Barefoot Investor* by Scott Pape. I cannot recommend this book highly enough. It bills itself as 'the only money guide you'll ever need' and it's true: straightforward, no bullshit, practical, specific and Australian. I have also signed up to Scott Pape's *Barefoot Blueprint* newsletter, which gives practical, independent advice so that you can go to a financial professional armed with concrete, well-informed suggestions.

6. Budgeting

Focus on the money you *save*, rather than the money you spend. Think of ways to make yourself a little wealthier every day. Of course, budgeting and saving are two sides of the same coin and it is important that you simply know what comes in and what goes out. Your budget needs to be kept updated and you should have it at your fingertips.

Don't think about 'a budget' as being restrictive. It is just information to ensure that you are waving, not drowning. In fact, in this budget there is a special section put aside for treats. Life is for living.

<u>Step 1</u> Have a guess at how much you spend over a month and over a year. Write it down. It is usually 25–50 per cent less than you really do.

<u>Step 2</u> Work out the real number. List all your income sources: salary, dividends, eBay sales etc. Then list all your outgoings/expenses. We live our lives forwards but understand them backwards – you need to work out how much you spend and what you spend it on. Get an online tracker (like the ones at sorted.org.nz or suzeorman.com), do an Excel spreadsheet or just buy an accounting notebook. There are also lots of templates online, which are useful as prompts to remember the less frequent, once-a-year expenses. Or try some of the budgeting apps now available, if they suit you.

✳

'An investment in knowledge pays the best interest.'
BENJAMIN FRANKLIN

Go through your last year of bank and credit card statements, line by line, group your purchases (food, clothing etc) and add the expenses to your budget. Print ATM receipts for a week and make a note of what you spend. Monitor the little things you usually buy with cash. It's not exactly a fun job but, once again, it is a means to an end.

Make your own list of outgoings:

- Mortgage or rent
- Loans
- Credit card interest
- Utilities (gas, electricity, water)
- Rates
- Doctor, dentist, optician, physio, prescriptions, medical expenses
- Mobile phone
- Computer maintenance, repairs, printer cartridges, domain names
- Car payment, insurance, rego, parking, petrol, servicing, repairs, tolls, fines, car wash
- Public transport
- Food, household items
- Alcohol (on a separate line as it can be cut down or out...)
- Dining out, take-aways, movies, theatre
- Hair, beauty
- Clothes, shoes, handbags, jewellery
- Household repairs
- Holidays, weekends away
- Insurance – health, house, contents
- Clubs, gym membership

- Books, subscriptions (Netflix, pay TV, magazines, i-Tunes)
- Pet expenses (food, vet, kennels, grooming)
- Gifts
- Hobbies
- Courses, night classes
- Charity donations
- Professional services (accountant, lawyer, financial advisor)

Be honest with yourself. You need to establish the true costs of everything.

<u>Step 3</u> Does your income cover your expenses? What is the gap? If there is a gap, how do you intend to fill it? Think about the 'wants' (new handbag) versus the 'needs' (food). You have two simple options: reduce your spending or bring in more income.

---- ✳ ----

'Money is the root of all evil, and yet it is such
a useful root that we cannot get on without it
any more than we can without potatoes.'

LOUISA MAY ALCOTT

7. How long will your money last?

Knowledge is power and once you know how much money you have and how much you spend and owe, work out how long your money would last if you stopped working tomorrow. Even if you are nervous about what you might uncover, just do it. Work out how much cash (liquid assets) you have right now, less any debts, and divide what is left by what you spend monthly. (This worst-case scenario assumes you'll never work again or get income from any other sources, such as selling your house or investments or a pension.) This figure will give you an indication of your financial health. Obviously you'd like the number to be as high as possible. Ten or 20 years is better than a matter of months. Even if it is only a few months, at least you know what you have to do. The fitness analogy springs to mind: 'eat less and exercise more' becomes 'reduce your costs and increase your income'.

After doing this calculation you might feel like bundling up your belongings in a red spotted hankie and chancing your luck in The Dark Forest, but *at least you know where you stand.* While the numbers can be confronting, they can also provide comfort in their concrete-ness. When my in-charge-of-the-money father died, my mother was all at sea, terrified she would not have enough to get by. We did this same calculation for her and established that, even if she had to move into a care home and sell her house, she would run out of money when she was around 120. In the event, she died with grace and dementia in her early eighties, but at the time it put her mind at rest.

If you find yourself having to fund years and years ahead, don't panic. Set a budget and seek advice from a reputable financial advisor to get you on track. (See section 10.) It might not be easy, and you may not be going on holiday in the foreseeable future, and you might have to do a job you don't particularly like and find yourself eating lots of tins of tuna, but at least you'll be in control. I'm willing to bet that whoever said, 'Choose your passion, not your pension' had an inheritance, a tidy divorce settlement or a trust fund! The rest of us just have to put our heads down and do what we have to do. (Still got to pay the mortgage, Oprah!)

8. Be smart with your money

The aim is to be financially organised and independent, living as you want (within sensible parameters), eventually without having to (or being able to) work. To achieve this you need to live within your means and generate a surplus to invest.

We have all become conditioned to expect a degree of comfort, even luxury, and many of our generation feel entitled to such a life. We are used to having the same 'toys' – phone, clothes, car, home, holidays – as our friends.

But we can't run with the pack on this one. Because of the significance of money when you live alone, because we are more vulnerable, we may not have a choice. We have to think twice about buying things we want but don't need. We need to save as much as we can. Every dollar spent now distances us a little from the life we want in the future.

'If passion drives you, let reason hold the reins.'

BENJAMIN FRANKLIN

Think like a millionaire. They are *much* more motivated by long-term financial security than by impressing anyone in the short term. It is really important that you run your own race financially. Depending on your circumstances, you may need to be more purpose-driven, sacrifice more and be more focused on where your money goes than your married friends. 'If you will live like no one else *now*, *later* you can live like no one else,' is the advice from Dave Ramsey, financial consultant. And Henry Thoreau argued that wealth should be defined not by how many *things* we have but by how much *free time* we have. So, the less you want or need, the 'richer' you are.

To help you get there:

- Make it a priority to pay off all your debts. Debt is bondage. Pay off your credit cards. Credit card debt is the most common cause of bankruptcy. And while you're at it, restrict yourself to only one credit card (*The Barefoot Investor* recommends getting rid of them all). Make sure it has a competitive rate of interest. Like most of us, I haven't got the time or the inclination to switch from card to card to get a better deal – usually if you ring your bank they will lower the interest rate if you say you're going to move.
- Work out how much you can afford to put into savings each month and make sure you contribute the maximum super allowed. Roll

'Frugality includes all the other virtues.'

CICERO

your super into one fund and make sure you are paying the lowest fees possible.

- Have an emergency fund that's readily accessible with a three to six month supply of money in it.

- Make your banking as simple as possible. Stick to one bank (the online banks offer the best deals) and close down superfluous accounts. Speak to the bank and make sure the accounts you have are the best ones for you.

- Thrift used to be considered a virtue, but isn't valued now. But the tide may be turning, given the success of the cheaper supermarkets such as Aldi – people who shop there consider themselves smart and canny, by paying lower prices without compromising on quality. I'm not interested in patronising you by telling you to do your washing in the off-peak middle of the night, switch to home brands or stop buying take-away coffees. You know better than anyone where your own 'low hanging fruit' is for quick, attainable savings. It's your call.

- The aim is to get money to invest and the two ways to achieve that are by increasing income or reducing consumption. A couple of simple thoughts that helped me put the brakes on were:

  ∗ Do you want that pair of shoes more than future security, an extra night on holiday, or those special taps in your future home?

  ∗ Imagine the money you're about to spend as seeds that you could instead plant (invest) to grow more money.

- The substantial savings lie with the *big* expenses. Too many of us pay what *Choice* magazine calls 'the lazy tax' by rolling over things like insurance, rather than looking for better deals. Treat it as a game and keep a tally sheet of how much you save. Be Robin Hood! The big corporations (electricity, mobiles) do not make it easy to change plans or clarify the differences between them, but persevere. At the end of the day it usually comes down to reading the small print in the PDS booklet, and many of the comparison sites are bogus.

Look at:

- Mortgage or rent – are you getting the best deal?
- Credit card. Slim down to one card only (no store cards) and get a card that has no fee, a lower interest rate or more rewards. Pay it off, in full, every month. If you are charged for a late fee payment, call up and ask for it to be waived.
- Check every credit card statement to ensure all charges are accurate. In 2016 Australians were scammed out of half a billion dollars. (When shopping online, make sure the website starts with https, not just http, to ensure security.)
- See if you can find cheaper utility and mobile phone providers. Compare energy plans at the government-run site Energy Made Easy.

———————————— ✳ ————————————

'Money is a terrible master but an excellent servant.'

P.T. BARNUM

- Don't just auto renew insurance without looking at alternative quotes, or at least speaking to your insurer on the phone to negotiate ways to reduce your bill (e.g. pay a higher excess). You could be paying for things you don't need, or perhaps not receiving a loyalty bonus. *The Barefoot Investor* quotes that only 7 per cent of Australians have the right level of insurance. Some companies will drop their price to keep you as a customer. Be careful, as some insurance companies offer a 'honeymoon' deal for a year, then bump up the price. Also, the quotes are rarely like-for-like, so you have to read the PDS booklets in excruciating detail to compare the policies – the top line two-page summary is not enough to compare. Be aware that sometimes it is worth paying a bit more for better service. (I have just taken my own advice and knocked almost $200 off my contents insurance, staying with the same company… so call!)
- For an independent comparison of private health policies go to privatehealth.gov.au.
- Sometimes paying bills with direct debit attracts a discount, but you have to weigh that up against increased vigilance with your statements to check what you are paying.
- Only withdraw money from an ATM that is free.
- Do the numbers on your car. Work out if it is cheaper in the long run to trade in your old car for a demo model or 'young' second-hand car, which will hold its value longer and not require major repairs. Do your homework online. At around the five-year mark car values depreciate rapidly. (My car has the zip and flair of a chest freezer, but is reliable and I have looked after it well, so I plan to keep it until it dies.)

For savings on smaller things:

- Stock up on genuine supermarket bargains. I have switched to shopping at Aldi, which is on average one-third cheaper than the other main supermarkets.
- Always check the unit price on the tag at the supermarket. Even if something is on sale, it doesn't always mean it's the cheapest option.
- Sign up to voucher and coupon sites but keep a separate email address for them so you don't get inundated. Look at ozbargain, for example.
- Look out for discount movie vouchers from telcos and health funds, use the discounts you get with your insurer and sign up to Lasttix, which sells last-minute tickets to plays and shows, sometimes reduced by 50 per cent.
- Before you buy from websites like Asos, check their social media sites for discount codes, or just google the company name + discount code. I got 30 per cent off my first internet order from a stationery company this way.
- You can get free cuts in hair salons that are looking for models (find them on Gumtree).
- Your money is too precious to give away. Hold onto it with the grip of a python. Don't lend money to anyone or agree to co-sign anything. 'No' is a complete sentence. Good relationships do not involve money.
- Finally, put aside a bit of 'treat' money so that you can splurge guilt free.

9. Saving and investing

This is where you reach a fork in the road. Once you have repaid debts, worked out your budget and simplified your banking, turn your thoughts to saving and investing. I am not a financial expert and this book can only give general advice, but investment is a key part of your Financial Blueprint. Along with *The Barefoot Investor*, the most straightforward 'understands me' book I have read on the subject is *A Man is Not a Financial Plan* by Joan Baker. Like *The Barefoot Investor*, it is written by an Australian for the local market so all the examples are relevant. Joan Baker outlines the three types of investment that deliver a passive income:

- Interest-bearing deposit accounts
- Business (including shares)
- Property

Which direction you take is up to you. Although they are not mutually exclusive, people tend to fall into one of two camps. There are those who spread savings around a range of investments, including deposits, bonds and super funds, which are reasonably safe and should

---

'Wealth consists not in having great possessions,
but in having few wants.'

EPICTETUS

increase wealth by a modest amount. Traditionally they would give a return of less than five per cent, but with interest rates so low at present, it could be much less. This is more savings than investment – small risk, small rewards.

As Robert G. Allen said: 'How many millionaires do you know who have become wealthy by investing in savings accounts? I rest my case.'

If you want to be more than just 'all right' and be *wealthy*, you need to take the other path and actively invest. That means buying and selling shares, or investing in property. Both have greater risks attached and you have to get cracking, as the sooner you get going the better. The longer you leave it, the harder it is to make substantial gains. You will also need to find people you really trust to help you.

One route isn't necessarily better than the other. You need to decide which is best for you, taking into account your age (the older you are, the less risk you can afford) and how actively you want to be involved.

If you choose to take the second route, it may involve borrowing. Most people who are serious about investing have to borrow. Obviously this decreases your disposable income in the short term (as you repay the loan plus interest) but will increase your capital in the long term as you can invest in assets you would not have been able to afford otherwise. I am wary of borrowing, but understand the concept of 'good borrowing' or 'good debt' – borrowing with the expectation of making a larger profit than if you hadn't.

In his book *Secrets of the Millionaire Mind* (it's better than it sounds!) T. Harv Eker goes as far as to say, 'I can't overemphasise the importance of creating passive income structures. It's simple. Without passive income you can never be free.' Gulp. Time to turn to the professionals.

10. Build a financial team

Finance is one area where it is definitely better not to go it alone when it comes to advice. Inform and arm yourself and then build a team of independent professionals to advise you – a financial advisor, an accountant (if you have a complicated tax return – otherwise do it yourself online with the ATO), a lawyer, plus, if necessary, a tax specialist, broker and risk adviser. Some people rely on the advice of friends: I wouldn't advise that, on so many levels. The best way to find a good accountant or financial advisor is usually through personal recommendation.

Assuming they are properly registered and accredited, you'll still need to interview your 'team', as independent professionals vary wildly in quality of advice and how they are remunerated (e.g. commission from the policies they sell, which will influence their advice). There are as many bad as good people in this area, so be very, very careful who you trust. It is also such a personal subject that I think it is important you have a rapport with your financial advisors. You will find lists of potential questions online or in books to ask

'Annual income twenty pounds, annual expenditure nineteen pounds nineteen and six, result happiness. Annual income twenty pounds, annual expenditure twenty pounds nought and six, result misery.'

MR MICAWBER IN *DAVID COPPERFIELD* BY CHARLES DICKENS

when you interview them. Go in with your eyes open and don't accept their advice or give them any money unless and until you feel completely comfortable. In order to get the best value from them, do as much of your own homework and preparation (your Financial Blueprint) in advance so that you make the most of the time you have with them, when the clock is ticking.

There are so many scammers out there. I learned the hard way. I fell foul of an unscrupulous financial advisor in London. I was sucked in because the company's point of difference was that they specialised in advising women. Ha! The empathetic female advisor was paid on commission and sold me several poor investments. I was too preoccupied with work to keep an eye on it and I lost a lot of money – which I could do with now! So *caveat emptor* or 'buyer beware'. I still kick myself for being so naive.

---- ✳ ----

'October: This is one of the peculiarly dangerous months to speculate in stocks. The others are July, January, September, April, November, May, March, June, December, August and February.'

MARK TWAIN, *PUDD'NHEAD WILSON*

11. Essential documents and backing up

- When you live by yourself, it is important that you have all of your documents up to date and make sure someone you trust knows where they are. Put them all together in a folder. No, I'm not thinking of the cat-eating-your-corpse-scenario, it's just common sense!

- Don't be one of the 50 per cent of the population who don't have a will. Do it. You will need to name your executor and beneficiaries. It's too important not to employ the State Trustees or a lawyer to write it. Keep a copy in a safe place. Your lawyer will also keep a copy.

- You'll also need to nominate an executor and enduring power of attorney to enable someone to act on your behalf in the event of mental incapacity. I have two old and trusted friends for this and have put money aside in my will to cover their costs. Add their details, along with your financial advisor, lawyer, accountant etc to the folder.

- Make sure you have specific nominations of who will receive your super. These names have to be restated every three years with your super provider.

- Keep your passports in the folder (photocopy the key pages and keep them separately), citizenship, legal documents such as birth certificate, and a photocopy of the contents of your wallet (all your cards).

- Keep separate lists of your bank accounts, super funds (and their binding nominations), shares (and share registry details) and the passwords to all your key sites. Change passwords regularly.

- Keep copies of all insurance policies in the folder.

- Don't forget to back up your computer and phone onto an external hard drive regularly. And for extra safety, back up your photos onto a USB stick. Every time I have been in the Apple store there is someone in tears because they didn't.
- I go through all these folders annually and keep them up to date. Feeling better organised?

12. Taking Action

When it comes to your finances, the 80:20 Pareto principle applies: successful finances are about 20 per cent knowledge and 80 per cent action. If you don't take any action at all, your financial situation will probably worsen, so even if you just change your super fund to one with a good track record and lower fees, you'll be ahead of the game. When you've finished reading this, get into gear. You have to actively manage your money and take an interest in it, because no one else will care as much as you do. I appreciate that it can be confronting and easy to postpone, but shift your mindset into 'confident' mode and in the space of a couple of hours you will have examined your optimal banking, super, insurer and other provider arrangements, your Financial Blueprint will be finished and you can have made some appointments with experts – and bought a copy of *The Barefoot Investor*! I can hardly think of anything more satisfying. Well done, you.

TAKE AWAYS

Being in control of your finances is critical, so write your Financial Blueprint.

Think: how you treat your money is a reflection of how you treat yourself. What is important to you? How do you feel about it? Adopt a positive, confident mindset.

Do: educate yourself. Write a budget. Work out how long your money will last.

Be smart with your money. Write a savings and investment plan. Build a team. Update your essential documents.

Take action right now!

Remind yourself that financial planning is the ultimate act of self-care.

Chapter 7

YOUR HOME

Look at your home with new eyes ∗ *Decoration ideas*
∗ *Key rooms* ∗ *Practicalities*

I'm sitting at my kitchen table, listening to the Sydney rain, and I am content. I love being at home. I have always been a strong believer that your surroundings have a profound impact on your wellbeing and that is multiplied a hundredfold when you live by yourself. It's not about how your home compares to the glossy spreads in an interiors magazine, or if you have a 'feature wall'. Your home embodies who you are and how you see yourself, how you spend time within its walls and how you care, nourish, wash and entertain yourself. As you get used to living *with* yourself not *by* yourself, you discover a whole world is enclosed in the word 'home'.

One of the many gifts of living alone is the possibility of getting to know (and design) our homes intimately and intricately. I know exactly where and how the light falls at different times of day, and can judge from the sound on the roof how hard the rain is falling. I know my home's creaks and foibles, and at night I can feel it breathe.

Naturally you want other people to like your place when they visit, but your focus shouldn't be on them. It is all about *you*, and how freeing is that? Your home is a statement *about* you (another litmus test of self-esteem) but even more it is a statement *to* you. It becomes as much an *idea* as a physical thing: your nest, your sanctuary, your rallying cry, your corner of the universe, your sounding board, therapy and a constant partner in transformation. The fourth-century hermit Abba Moses said, 'Go, sit in your cell, and your cell will teach you everything'. Maybe our homes can teach us too.

Being at home alone isn't a last resort. You are *somewhere* – your place. And you are with *someone who matters* – you.

A starting point

Find a quiet spot in your home and sit for 10 minutes soaking up the atmosphere. Can you feel its energy? Is it positive or negative? If it's positive, that's great. If it's negative, you can change that straight away by laughing out loud, meditating, or smudging with a sage stick. (Don't just dismiss this as bullshit: it works!) Think about how you want to feel in your home. You'll want different things at different times, but what are the most important? To feel safe, comfortable, happy, energised, calm, restored, busy, loved, content, relaxed, productive, comforted, transformed, inspired, nurtured, at ease or at peace? Choose what are most important to you. Hopefully they will align with the atmosphere in your home. If not, consider what you can change.

Location, location, location

Does where you live – city, country or suburbia – allow you to live the way you want to?

Budget, proximity to work, family, friends and lifestyle are the basic criteria. After that, we have three choices – city, country or suburbia. The city has the advantage of varied activities at your fingertips and sheer numbers of people, but sometimes it can give you less of a connection to neighbours or community. In the country the community tends to be closer, with people looking out for one another, but you could also be potentially isolated and have fewer opportunities to meet new people – and everyone knows your business! For many single people living alone, suburbia can be a no man's land of happy families. But it's horses for courses and you will know what is feasible and right for you. Don't get stuck in a rut. You can always move!

The same goes for size – obviously we all have financial constraints, but is the size of your home right for how you live? If you don't entertain often, do you need the space for a dining table or separate eating area? If you work from home, are you happy to work in your kitchen (as I do) or bedroom, or do you need extra space to write or create? (A good friend rented a particular house specifically so that she could use the garage as her studio.) I have many divorced and widowed friends who have been forced to downsize but they don't care, because the opportunity to express themselves anew outweighs the fact that the washing machine and dryer are stacked in the bathroom and they need pointe ballet shoes to get around without knocking things over. One woman described the sensation of having her own space as 'a whole house full of fresh air'. Another friend painted every floor white, just because she could.

171

The point is that most of us can decide where we live, so make it somewhere you want to be, in a size that works for you. Don't be afraid to move. Of course it is nerve racking, but for many women it has provided exactly the boost they need to kick start a new stage of their life.

Welcome to my home

It's not just a change of location that offers an end to stagnation. Simply changing something in your home can have the same effect.

Look at your home with fresh eyes. What do you see? Imagine you were doing a tour of your home for a TV show or YouTube video. Make a quick video of yourself 'presenting' on your phone and try it out: 'Here I am in my kitchen, with everything at hand. This is where I write my emails and here is my reading seat, my cosy bedroom…' and so on. Which bits are you proudest of, which bits work and which parts do you gloss over? The over-stacked shelves you've been meaning to go through? The chipped paint you have been meaning to fix? The ugly chair you've been meaning to replace? Bulging wardrobes? Paperwork covering every surface?

Think about how you would like the space to look and superimpose it on space you live in now: a mental before and after. Sometimes it's

---

*

'Your house is your larger body. It grows in the sun and sleeps in the stillness of the night; and it is not dreamless.'

KAHIL GIBRAN

minor tweaks; sometimes it's a bit more involved. But this is not about hiring a fancy decorator or a big renovation. The smallest adjustments can have a huge impact. Change gives you energy, but make sure it is a reflection of *you*, not a standard, taupe, cookie-cutter nightmare from a TV renovation reality show.

How do you use your space?

Your home should fit around you and your needs, not the other way around. How do you use your home? Of course it is your sanctuary, but it is also a place to have friends over, and possibly work in too. It's worth weighing up the different parts of your life to see if your home dovetails and delivers. For example, one friend with a very stressful job relies purely on her home to recharge her. So she boldly transformed the second bedroom into a breathtaking Balinese-inspired bathroom. Good for resale value? Possibly not. Nourishing for her soul? Absolutely. Another friend who works from home simply moved her desk into a spot with more natural light and invested in a proper work chair, shelving and desk lamp – huge improvement. If you enjoy cooking, how can you optimise your kitchen space?

If you are lucky enough to love your home exactly the way it is – you feel it fits you like a custom pair of Christian Louboutins – then skip the next few paragraphs. But if not, stay with me…

Find your home's 'desire paths'

Shape your home around the way you live by identifying its 'desire paths'. A 'desire path' in urban planning is a path created by pedestrians as a common-sense shortcut to avoid the longer route on the tarmacked footpath. We all know a few. According to Wikipedia: 'In Finland, planners are known to visit their parks immediately after the first snowfall, when the existing paths are not visible. People naturally choose desire paths, clearly marked by their footprints, which can be then used to guide the routing of new purpose-built paths.' Brilliant.

Think about the 'desire paths' in your house. What are the things that can be moved or changed to be close at hand and make your life easier? Line up your morning routine essentials on the right hand side of the bathroom basin if you're right handed, or put your go-to recipes in a separate folder, or rejig the cutlery drawer so that your favourite knives, forks and spoons are in a separate slot. Untangle and organise your charging cords. If your reading chair needs a footstool, a throw, or better lighting, see to it.

Inspiration for decoration

Even if you don't intend to change the decor of your home, it is worth trawling for inspiration, even if it's just for a couple of small ideas. You can follow your nose, or articulate the style you're after. Would it be comfortable, functional, stylish, minimalist, eclectic, vintage, beautiful, unusual, quirky, homely, inspired, unique, individual, modest, simple, traditional, graceful, creative, mellow or atmospheric?

Then hop on the internet, look at Pinterest or Houzz or one of the many other home decor sites, and use the search function to narrow it down, making pinboards as you go. Sooner or later you'll find someone posting who has a similar vibe to you and before you know it you'll have an inspirational board with loads of ideas. Or buy just one interiors magazine and look at it imaginatively, stealing a few small details, like using a trophy as a vase, or leaning pictures in front of books on your bookshelf.

Choosing colours

Living alone allows you the opportunity to explore your creative side in many different ways and choosing the colour of your walls is one of them. I'm not advocating every room should be a different colour – nearly all of mine are white – but a dash of colour goes a long way. You might think you don't know where to start, but you do!

- Looking back at your Pinterest boards, do certain colours keep appearing?
- Buy a colour swatch from a smaller paint company where someone with a trained eye has curated a collection, such as Porter's Paints. The smaller selection makes decision-making much easier.
- You are instinctively drawn to certain colours. Walk around your house and pinpoint the colours of the things you love. A favourite outfit, a vase, a bowl, a painting or a cushion.
- For perfect colour combinations, look to nature. Books of birds, butterflies and fish will reveal incredible juxtapositions of colours that are perfect. The shot of yellow in the pristine white of a sulphur crested cockatoo, or the pink, black and white of a turtledove, or the hues of a blue swimmer crab.

---
*

'Ah! There is nothing like staying at home for real comfort.'

JANE AUSTEN, *EMMA*

- Go for a walk and really look at things… rust on a gate, the weathered wood of an old door, the colours of an old shop sign or oil in a puddle. Take photos.

After a while you'll notice that you are drawn to the same colours or combinations. For me, it's white and the palest blue, which ended up being the colour of my bedroom ceiling. Every day when I wake up, I love it.

Some good interiors websites
- pinterest.com
- houzz.com
- elementsilove.com
- greigedesign.com
- missmustardseed.com
- funkyjunkinteriors.net
- inspiredbarn.com
- mysweetsavannahblog.com
- surfaceview.co.uk
- idealhome.co.uk

A few ideas from my scrapbooks:
- Look carefully at what possessions you already have and think about ways to rearrange them into different groups and combinations. It's more about mergers than acquisitions!
- Have flowers on your bedside table. The vase can be anything that holds water, such as a beautiful tin can, a cup and saucer, or an old milk jug.

- Bring outdoor garden statues inside. There are often amazing bargains in garden centres. (Then google how to give them a patina.)
- Create collections of objects – vases, hats, baskets, the boards from old board games, and so on.
- Paint writing on the wall – a favourite phrase printed out, traced and painted looks wonderful and unique.
- Wallpaper one wall. Some of the wallpapers available now are truly beautiful. Look on Pinterest for inspiration – narrow the results in the search e.g. 'wallpaper with birds'.
- Go to your local flea market and wait to be drawn to something with a bit of patina that tells a story.
- Arrange fruit and veg in bowls on the table instead of flowers when you're having friends over.
- Hide something in each room that makes you smile – an old, loved teddy bear hidden among your clothes, a photo of you with a friend inside a cupboard door, a tiny butterfly water-coloured on the wall behind a curtain, favourite postcards stuck inside your wardrobe doors, or beautiful paper lining your clothing drawers.

———————————— ✳ ————————————

'He is happiest, be he king or peasant, who finds peace in his home.'
GOETHE

- Have flowers and plants in interesting pots. (Outside I have cheated and incorporated fake ones from Ikea that look great!)
- Print out photos of trips and frame them or make them into collages with tickets, maps and keepsakes.
- Surround yourself with pictures of people who love you.
- Order letterhead writing paper or cards printed with your address (these also make a fantastic gift).

KEY ROOMS

Which room(s) you want to prioritise? Tizz them up *one at a time.* It is so much more satisfying to have one room finished than several half-finished. (Multi-tasking is a myth.)

- Your entrance
- Your bedroom
- Your living room
- Your kitchen
- Your bathroom

'The home should be the treasure chest of living.'
LE CORBUSIER

Your entrance

Oprah nailed it when she said your home should 'rise up to greet you'. More often than not you'll be coming home alone, so put some thought into the entrance of your home to make sure it welcomes you.

Are you happy with the lighting, door knocker, handle, bell and mat? I found a beautiful old metal door knocker of a hand holding a ball in a junk shop in Tunisia and I love it. Or how about a metal sign or mat saying 'welcome', with a plant by the door? Small touches, but they all add up. Think about the colour of your door. If you are allowed to paint it (i.e. you're not renting or in an apartment block), make sure you paint it a colour you love. There are plenty of apps and digital programs where you can try out different colours superimposed on a photograph of your place. I have a fire-engine red door (chosen by my daughter) and it lifts my spirits every day. I also have a small tree in a pot by the entrance.

In your hallway, think about having a light on a timer switch so that you always come home to brightness. Hang photos of friends and family to welcome you in, along with a slim table or shelf for keys and post and a flower in a vase. You deserve to have your spirits lifted as you enter.

To avoid any 'something-about-Mary' moments, hang a mirror so you can double-check before you go out, to catch the spinach in your teeth or the blob of yoghurt on your chin.

Your bedroom

Your private HQ and base camp; another area of privacy, retreat and sanctuary. It's the most personal space in your home and the place to recharge your batteries. Start with your bed. No his or her side of the bed: it's all yours, baby. *Blissonastick!* As for Shakespeare famously leaving his wife his 'second best bed' in his will. Pah! Get the best bed you can afford. One friend has just bought the four-poster she always wanted. Like your sofa, it's worth the investment and you'll never regret the outlay. I think of my bed as an oasis – a big, soft, white, snowy, feathery island of retreat. I say 'retreat'… some nights I just keel over like a piece of old timber.

The same principal of investment goes for sheets, doona, doona covers, pillowcases, blankets and throws. Look online to find your favourites and wait until they go on sale. I only have white linens, which I adore. For hotel luxury, consider a mattress topper (mattress pad or featherbed) that goes over your mattress. In summer I sleep under a very patched old soft linen sheet that belonged to my mother, topped off with a cotton knit blanket. When I remember, I use a lovely citrus linen spray when they are hanging on the washing line. In winter I heat the bed with an electric blanket and snuggle up with a couple of those velvety plush throws on top – it's like sleeping under a prone teddy bear.

Sleep on the pillows of a millionaire. If you're going to spend a third of your life with your face pressed against it, make sure you love it. Invest in the very best: it's a relatively small outlay for a huge payback.

Check out hotel websites where they might sell their bedding. In theory, if you sleep on your side you should have a firm pillow, if you sleep on your back, a medium pillow, and if you're a front-down sleeper you should opt for a soft pillow. Hunt around, choose what you want, but make sure you love it.

It is a nice idea to assign your day an adjective as your feet touch the floor when you first get out of bed ('calm', 'productive', 'energetic' and so on). For a bit of added luxury, place a small rug beside your bed that is warm on your feet in winter and cool in summer, just like they do in really good hotels. If it's good enough for the Ritz, it's good enough for me.

Some people sleep with their pets on the bed. I don't. Rory my dog sleeps at the foot of my bed, on the floor. He's not allowed on the bed (or sofa) at all. My space! (Although I know that sometimes when I'm not here he sneaks up and writhes around on my bed in bliss like an overacting pornstar. Muddy footprints provide the evidence.) Dogs snore (and fart!) – who knew? Not me. I thought I'd done with that, but ex's nightly snoring has been replaced by Rory's fortissimo canine rumbles.

———————————— ✳ ————————————

'Home interprets heaven. Home is heaven for beginners.'

CHARLES HENRY PARKHURST

Have a full-length mirror in your bedroom, for a final check before you go out. It's a better option than having the bus driver tell you your dress is in your knickers, or your shirt buttons are done up wonkily. I have lost track of the times I got dressed in the dark and sallied forth with clothes inside out, or wearing one black and one blue shoe.

Search online again for inspirational ways to make your bedroom more special. Make sure the bedside table is clear of clutter but big enough to hold a good reading light, water bottle, book, tissues, candle, notebook and pen, your journal, picture frame, flowers, torch – whatever you want and need. I have two clocks – one on each bedside table, so that I don't have to turn over in the middle of the night to find out the time – a good example of a 'desire path' in action. I have a tiny ceramic angel that a friend gave me and a welcoming string of (battery-powered) mini fairy lights on a copper wire around the antique French shutters that serve as my bedhead.

The last thing you see at night and the first thing you wake up to should be positive and life affirming. One strip of wall in my bedroom is covered in Canite (like pinboard), to provide a constantly changing vision board. I've installed narrow shelves by my bed, which are full of framed photos of family, friends and favourite places. It is comforting

'Run a home like you would a small business and treat it with the same seriousness.'

ANTHEA TURNER

to know that on the nights I lie awake worrying, on nights so dark I feel surrounded by black velvet, they are watching over me.

It's nice to perform a little ritual at night – maybe spray your pillow with scent (my top three are Jo Malone's Lime, basil and mandarin cologne, Eau de Rochas and Eau d'Hadrien by Annick Goutal), listen to some music, flick on a flameless candle, read a few pages of a book and contemplate the day just gone.

I don't have much of a view from my bedroom – I look over the row of terraced houses opposite – but sometimes the sky is a beautiful colour or I'll have a guest appearance from a cockatoo. I like to capture the same view in different seasons, at different times of day. My personal view.

Your living room

Invest in a sofa you love. It is a key piece, so try not to compromise. Dress it up with eclectic cushions and, if you're handy with a sewing machine, make some more from material you like or embroider your name or a phrase that's meaningful for you. (Write it freehand, then go over it in cable stitch – YouTube it!) Etsy also has some great cushions. I also have a velvety soft throw that I cuddle up in (and a lightweight cotton one for summer), plus a good reading lamp so that there is always a cosy place to read. In terms of knick knacks and paintings, only have what pleases you. It is lovely to own things that are hand made: it could just be a simple bowl, or a sketch done by a student at your nearest art college (go the final shows and snap up a bargain). It is just something unique to you and your home.

You have the opportunity to surround yourself with things that appeal to you on a visceral level. If you have ever been to a 'Body Talk' session, you will know that your body instinctively reacts in a certain way. It is drawn to some things and pulls back from others. Surround yourself with things you are drawn to. One friend, for example, is drawn to Wabi-sabi – a Japanese decorative philosophy based on small pleasures, which honours the handcrafted in all its imperfections. Matsuo Basho, the poet, combined the words *wabi* ('lonely') and *sabi* ('rust') to explain 'the taste for the simple and the quiet'. Look at things piece by piece and weigh up if they have earned a place in your home.

Also (and stay with me on this one), think about ditching your TV altogether. I do understand that some people see it as 'company' and like the sound of it in the background to fill the silence. But it can be such a time thief, and is becoming more and more redundant in the age of Netflix and playback TV on a laptop. I am not suggesting you become a Trappist nun and eschew technology altogether, but with a laptop you aren't tied to the sofa – you can watch in bed, or while you are cooking. For this reason I am also a big fan of radio. With the internet, you can now listen to radio stations and podcasts from all over the world.

Music can also play an important role in your home. It's useful to have a good-quality portable Bluetooth speaker that you can move from room to room, and it's even better if you keep finding new music that rocks your boat. Ask your friends and look on the internet, then make playlists for all your different moods – put all your CDs on your computer and then back it up. And don't just limit yourself to music.

Some of my favourite tracks include the sound of rainfall and Korean monks chanting. Once you've set it up, you can have the same song on repeat until your ears bleed, and there's no one to complain.

Your kitchen

What goes on in your kitchen has a direct correlation to your self-worth, but it's an easy place to let things slip. After all, who's to know, right? Letting the dirty dishes pile up, ignoring a spill on the floor, eating standing up from a takeaway container with a spork, and not clearing out the freezer or taking the rubbish out as often as you should? Sounds familiar? Along with the bathroom, this room has to be spotlessly, operating-theatre clean. Each of us has a line in the sand that, if crossed, means we've gone too far. For me that's leaving the washing up. I feel that if that slips my whole house will look like the aftermath of a sorority party, or a hoarder's paradise.

As mentioned earlier, I look forward to the ritual of eating by myself in the evening. Because I also work at my small square kitchen table,

---

✳

'A house is not a home unless it contains food and fire
for the mind as well as the body.'

BENJAMIN FRANKLIN

I mark the end of the working day by putting a tablecloth on it (or just a nice vintage linen tea towel), lighting a candle, and setting a place, complete with a table napkin in a silver ring. Small effort, big reward. I have a selection of homemade tablecloths; one made from old tea towels stitched together, another just a hemmed length of material that caught my eye. They sit folded in a basket, ready to go.

If you are lucky enough to own nice china and cutlery, use them every day. If not, buy a setting just for you. In the past few years I have picked up odd pieces of tableware, ranging from bowls beautifully decorated with fish and octopuses (or is that octopi?) to divided bento plates from Muji to a thin and beautiful aubergine-coloured noodle bowl from Mud to a salad plate shaped like a lettuce leaf. And lots of blue and white plates and bowls from Chinatown and Japanese shops. And blue and white enamel Falcon Ware. And mini wooden chopping boards, on which I plonk my food à la Jamie Oliver. I just love them. The same goes for glasses, which I pick up, one at a time, from charity, junk and antique shops. As 'orphans' they are not expensive. This is about the only time when buying for one is a bargain!

Take a step back for a minute – literally. Are you happy with the way your kitchen looks? Just because it's a kitchen doesn't mean it can't have paintings (although nothing valuable, of course, because of the grease from cooking) or photographs of your favourite faces and places. If you

'Home is where one starts from.'

T.S. ELIOT

spend a lot of time in your kitchen, as I do, it is worth putting in a proportionate amount of thought as to how it looks and feels. When I have a few friends over, everyone ends up sitting on high stools in the kitchen and chatting as I cook, or eating at the little table. I have a couple of big pinboards covered in tickets, photos, cards, letters, vintage price labels (bought on eBay), paper fans and dragons from Chinatown. They provide great conversation starters. I also have framed collages of photographs from holidays with the children. These keep the memories alive and make me smile every time I walk past. Photographs do not belong on memory cards: they only have currency once we print them, or use them as wallpaper on our devices.

Your bathroom

There is barely a woman alive whose pupils don't dilate at the words 'beautiful bathroom'. It's often the first thing we check out in a hotel room, a newly renovated house or a real estate viewing. Having a beautiful private space in which to clean, relax, soak and recalibrate – not to mention pluck, brush, squeeze, poke and prod – is very important.

The three most important elements of a bathroom for someone living alone are good lighting, a magnifying mirror and a bath.

Lighting and a magnifying mirror go together. There is no one else to point out your mascara panda eyes or tell you your eyebrows need a hedge trimmer, or even that you look unwell. You have to see it and fix it, and to do that you need decent lighting and a good mirror – end of

187

story. I had extra lights installed, including two heat lamps, and bought a magnifying mirror (a round one on an extending arm – just $15 at a storage shop). It's possibly the best $15 I've ever spent. Or buy a magnifying mirror with built-in light – once you have one of those babies, there's no going back.

Bath, bath, bath – let me count the ways I love you. When I was growing up in England, showers barely existed and were considered quite exotic. So a bath is normal to me. In fact, it is a deal-breaker when renting or buying a home. No bath, no contract. And yes, of course you need a shower in the morning, but I have a bath almost every night and it's got nothing to do with getting clean. It's a metaphor for renewal. I am slightly embarrassed to admit that I even have a Pinterest board of beautiful baths and have fantasised that in my parallel universe life, where money is no object, I'll do a tour of the world's best hotel baths. They all have views: of the Taj Mahal from a bath in the Oberoi in Agra, to an aquarium from a bath in Dubai's Atlantis Hotel. But I digress. I know baths are not essential, but neither are candles and flowers and champagne and bitter dark chocolate. And on reflection, don't they go well together?

When you live alone your bathroom assumes an important role as your self-care hub, your spa, your treat and your indulgence. What can you do to make the existing space more enticing? I just searched 'spa bathroom' on Pinterest and there were lots of great ideas, from 'how to hotel-ify your bathroom' to 'how to turn your bathroom into a spa experience'.

A few small touches can make all the difference. Candles (nowhere near your hair!) or flameless candles, some bubble bath (I still think Badedas can't be beaten, although I put it in after the bath has run), a luxurious bath mat, a bath pillow, a headband, a beautiful robe (I bought mine from a spa I visited), goodies in baskets, a body brush, a natural sea sponge, some relaxing background music and a stash of tiny bars of chocolate so that I can eat one in the bath. And yes, you'll need a back scratcher. I always have at least two towels on the go to guarantee a dry one, plus a few white ones folded in a pile (the quickest way to that luxury hotel look) and a black wash cloth (so no make-up on those white towels). The one little thing that makes the biggest difference to the look and energy of the room is a little bunch of fresh flowers. Or just a single bud. Give it a try.

What should you keep in your medicine cabinet? Because you are your own first-aider, make sure your bathroom cabinet is well stocked with everything you might need, including bandaids, headache pills, cough and cold medicine, throat lozenges, bandages, thermometer, antihistamine, antiseptic cream, mozzie bite ointment, hydrogen peroxide for splinters, sunscreen, tweezers, scissors, spare toothbrush, diarrhoea and constipation pills, rehydration salts, cotton buds and tissues. Check the use-by dates regularly. If you are on medication, there are lots of apps that will help you manage them.

Finally, don't get locked in! Make sure the handle and lock on your bathroom door is in good nick. A dodgy lock can mean you're trapped, even if you just shut the door without actually locking it. Trust me, I learned the hard way!

'Collect moments, not things.'
AUTHOR UNKNOWN

PRACTICAL UPKEEP

Happiness comes from being engaged in life, not acquiring and having more stuff. In other words, as has often been quipped: 'Never cry over anything that can't cry over you.'

Clutter

I nurture a delusion that one day my house will be a clutter-free zone but the chances are slimmer than Kate Moss. Nevertheless, I do my best to tame it on an ongoing basis, so that I am in control of it, not the other way round. If I don't clear it, no one else will.

It is easy to subscribe to the notion that an uncluttered space allows you to breathe in every sense of the word. Decluttering expert Peter Walsh puts it very well: 'Things that are left undone can be your own undoing. They just add stress and waste precious time. Organising is the act of giving yourself more time and peace of mind.' I agree, but even as I write, out of the corner of my eye I can see papers and books creeping like triffids over every flat surface. Sometimes I feel like

---

Home is a name, a word, it is a strong one;
stronger than magician ever spoke, or spirit ever
answered to, in the strongest conjuration.'

CHARLES DICKENS, *MARTIN CHUZZLEWIT*

putting the whole lot in the dustbin and seeing if there are any repercussions. A friend said that when she moved from the UK to Australia a little bit of her wished her container would fall off the ship so that she could start again with less stuff. I get that.

So how to get motivated? I try to stick to the rule that when something comes into the house, something goes out. New things need to earn the right to be in your life. The artist and textile designer William Morris said: 'Have nothing in your house that you do not know to be useful, or believe to be beautiful.' I have found the best way to attack clutter is to deal with a small bit at a time – three piles of papers or a couple of shelves – half an hour every day. I see myself as a character in the *The Great Escape,* tunnelling out the earth (clutter) bit by bit. Once a month I take a load to the charity shop.

Tidying and cleaning

Living alone offers freedom but also calls for a level of self-discipline. If you leave your wet towel on the bathroom floor it will lie there like a slug, unloved and unmoving, indefinitely. The best way to keep the place tidy is to pretend that someone – a friend, a real estate agent – is about to drop in, so it needs to be in good nick.

The same goes for cleaning. I put aside a day a week when the house gets hoovered and jiffed – guest ready. Between times, the bathroom and kitchen floors get mopped and the loos cleaned. Clean windows make a huge difference too. About once a year I have the carpets and sofa steam cleaned and the house sprayed for insects. I was coy when I wrote that. By 'insects' I really mean cockroaches, and where I live in Sydney you could put a saddle on them.

Security

You must feel 100 per cent secure in your home. Questions like 'Could someone break in at night or while I am out?' or 'Will I be burgled?' are not your friends. If you are not confident about your security, get a locksmith to upgrade the locks on your main doors, plus add a peephole, door chain, window locks and bars if necessary. Get a burglar alarm installed and use it. I have a lovely heavy old bolt on the front door that I clink shut every night and it gives me extra reassurance. Put signs and stickers around the outside of the property advising that you have a burglar alarm (and a dog if you have one). If you have precious jewellery, always hide it – and not in your sock drawer. You can buy small safes camouflaged as tins of food, books or even electricity sockets. There are some good home security apps available that can do everything from monitoring home from your phone, to turning your home computer into a surveillance system, to switching your lights on and off while you are out. They are upgrading all the time, so check out what suits you.

Other security hints include making it look as though more than one person lives at your place by having multiple pairs of shoes visible, including some men's, installing motion detector outdoor lights, never putting personal details on your key ring and being careful who you give spare keys to. If you get your car washed or serviced, or extra keys cut, always detach them from the main set. Know your neighbours so that they can keep an eye out for you, especially if you're going away. Never order a taxi from your house if you are going to the airport; give a different address nearby and wait there.

Make sure you have a working torch and a supply of candles and matches, along with a fire blanket and small fire extinguisher in the kitchen. Have fire alarms properly installed and check them regularly (when the clocks change). Candles create a lovely atmosphere, but be very, very careful of them. If you light them at night and are alone, set an alarm to ensure you don't fall asleep with them burning. Better still, try flameless candles – they are more and more lifelike.

Do it yourself

Sometimes I feel like a human Swiss Army Knife… She sews! She drills! She unblocks sinks! She hammers! She can take stones out of horses' hooves! The reality is that being alone means you have to step up and become adept at basic home maintenance. DIY takes on a whole new meaning when *everything* is bloody DIY. If you let things slide, maintenance-wise, you will usually have a bigger and more expensive headache waiting for you down the track. 'Look after your home and it will look after you' is the theory. I have always been quite good at electrical matters and can handle blackouts with aplomb. I have also taught myself to Gerni the yard, plunge the loo, replace a washer on a leaking tap, drill a hole to hang a picture, fix the hot water system, clean the filters on the cooker hood and air conditioner, replace the seals on the fridge, clean the gutters, reboot the alarm system, replace the batteries in the smoke detectors, grout and paint bathroom tiles, kill cockroaches, pantry moths and even mice, fix the internet and descale the showerheads.

Of course there are some jobs I can't do by myself – hang heavy pictures, anything involving climbing up a huge ladder, or move heavy furniture (although you can get slider gizmos). Use your common sense and err on the side of caution. I keep an onging list of jobs in a book in the kitchen and when it gets long enough I'll call in a handyman for half a day. And of course I employ an expert for roofing, major electrical and plumbing work. I know my limitations!

It's worth investing in good tools (the same goes for kitchen equipment). Forget about the patronising downsized toolsets with patterned handles aimed at women. What were they thinking? You'll need a good-size walloping claw hammer, tape measure, nails, screws, picture hanging hooks, super glue, a proper screwdriver with different heads – Phillips and normal – duct tape, masking tape, paint brushes, awl, selection of batteries, pliers, wrench, level, small saw, utility knife, plunger, drill and upholstery stapler. Phew. I keep all my tools in one drawer. I also have an 'electricity drawer', containing socket extensions, light bulbs, timer switches, plugs for different countries, leads and so on.

TAKE AWAYS

Your home has a disproportionate
impact on your wellbeing.

Articulate its energy and look at
the space with new eyes.

Find the 'desire paths'
in your home.

Don't be afraid of colour.

Go through your home, room by
room, and incorporate some of
the ideas in this chapter, taking
additional inspiration from the
internet and magazines.

Stay on top of practicalities such
as clutter, tidying, cleaning,
security, DIY and maintenance.

Make sure you love the
space you're in.

Chapter 8

DOING THINGS
BY YOURSELF

Travelling * *Christmas* * *Restaurants* * *Cinema*
* *Make the most of your time alone*

Living alone is not an excuse to miss out on anything and everything you want to do – and the satisfaction of doing them is all the sweeter. It's a question of opening the door and making your own adventures. I am still taken aback by how many of my non-solo friends have a simultaneously smug and morbid curiosity about how I manage to go on holiday, to a concert, a gallery, the movies, or – heaven forbid – to eat at a restaurant by myself. 'I could never do that,' they murmur. Of course they could. The enormous elephant in the corner of the room is just the fear of awkwardness, embarrassment, being judged, labelled odd, lonely and friendless or simply not enjoying it.

News flash. No. One. Cares. It is a well-known fact that 100 per cent of humanity is 100 per cent self-absorbed. Your fellow diners are thinking about how they hate the way their husband chews his food, or wishing they'd ordered what their friend ordered, or weighing up whether the carbonara is WTC (Worth The Calories), or thinking how noisy the restaurant is, or why Jo didn't text back, or they'd rather be at home watching Netflix… they are not wondering why you are sitting there alone. No one cares. People don't judge, draw conclusions, or speculate. They don't think about you at all, or even if they do, so what? It's more and more common to see solos getting on with their lives. Life goes on. I love travelling, movies and eating out, plus there are a couple of classes I have my eye on. Why should I miss out because I haven't got someone to go with?

Your future is shaped by what you do today, tomorrow and the next day, so make some plans, open your front door and step out with your head held high.

'Just' give it the flick

I catch myself saying it all the time. '*Just* one ticket, please.' 'A table *just* for one, please.' '*Just* one slice, please.' 'Just': a diminishing word, along with 'only' (as in 'only one, please'). Why do we apologise? Because we're not worth the trouble? We teach others how to treat us and saying 'just' sets people up to treat you differently. I try to remove it from my lexicon. I am one, and one is enough.

The first part of this chapter is about navigating events by yourself. The second is about how to make the most of your time alone.

'The things one experiences alone with oneself are
very much stronger and purer.'

EUGENE DELACROIX

PART 1 NAVIGATING EVENTS

By 'events' I mean holidays, cinema, eating out, Christmas and long weekends. I try to balance my diary by booking in some dates in advance – a concert or play, a course, a holiday, and a weekend away with friends or by myself. They act like markers in the ground – some pegs to hang the year on and anticipate – while allowing plenty of time for impulsivity.

Solo travelling (or 'Glad you're not here')

I am biased. Travelling has a special place in my heart. I love it, and (or is that 'but'?) it is also the ultimate test of how much you like yourself and how happy you *really* are being alone. Travelling by yourself is not always easy, but offers great rewards. You discover who you are when no one else is looking.

Agatha Christie captured the spirit of travel beautifully: 'Your travel life has the aspect of a dream. It is something outside the normal, yet you are in it. It is peopled with characters you have never seen before and in all probability will never see again. It brings occasional homesickness, and loneliness, and pangs of longing ... But you are like the Vikings who have gone into a world of adventure, and home is not home until you return.'

Spread your wings and fly

Most people you know won't 'get' travelling alone, but I am prepared to bet that most of them have never tried it. It pays to have a thick skin. Last year I was planning a trip to France and took language classes to polish up my schoolgirl *français*. When I revealed my plans, a fellow student chimed in, 'But won't you be really lonely going to Paris by yourself? The city of love?' Thanks for that, sister. The mental riposte was, 'If you can rustle me up a tall bloke who can spell, cheerfully eat his bodyweight in *palourdes farçies* (stuffed clams) and gets irony, then I'll take him. If not, I'll be fine by myself, thank you very much.' And so I was. Off I went to Paris (and Dubai and Rome and Normandy and Noirmoutier) and I loved every second.

Trust me. If you have doubts about travelling solo, cast them aside, spread your wings and fly. Travelling by myself has been a revelation. I have learned what I like and don't like (roof terraces and crowds respectively), my level of tolerance for average food, heat and queues (not high) and how to pace myself (full-on in the mornings, chillin' in the afternoons). I have a proclivity for markets, street food and dusty old stationery shops. I favour small cities and minor museums. I have also learned that I have pockets of strength, confidence, curiosity and resilience that I never knew.

On the down side, your suspicions are correct. The travel industry is designed and rigged for couples and families. You will usually pay the same amount as a couple for a hotel room, a place on a tour or cruise, travel insurance and car hire. Seek out one of the increasing numbers of travel agents and tour operators who specialise in solo travellers and guarantee no single supplements. Time spent shopping around is always time well spent.

'Time is a bird; it perches then it flies.'
AUTHOR UNKNOWN

Another natural concern when travelling alone is security. Of course the threat of random terrorism casts a long shadow, but I am quite philosophical about that risk. Don't be a chicken and confine yourself to a resort – branch out, but be sensible when choosing your destination, and always follow government travel advice. Do your homework about safety from Lonely Planet and other guides, travel blogs etc. Avoid any 'rough parts of town' (they are often around major train stations) and be vigilant at night. Common sense is your best guide and always heed the advice of the locals. If you are really nervous, consider taking a basic self-defense course.

At the risk of sounding like a stuck record (remember them?), how you approach your trip will determine your level of enjoyment. If you are jittery and apprehensive, seeing your solo trip as a compromise, then that is exactly what it will be. If you view it as an exciting adventure where you get to hold the reins, observe, grow, meet interesting people and experience new sensations then that is exactly what will happen.

We are lucky because travelling *with* yourself (rather than *by* yourself) has never been easier or more accepted. The stigma of travelling alone is dissolving in the face of the inexorable rise of confident solo travellers who are showing how it's done. A great resource is the *Solo Traveler* blog, with plenty of advice about different destinations and practical tips from fellow soloists. I would also thoroughly recommend their book, *The Solo Traveler's Handbook*.

Before you leave

Collect inspiration for possible destinations whenever you find it. I keep scrapbooks (one digital, one physical) of places I read or hear about that I'd like to go to one day. I also have a map of the world and circle places I want to visit. If you haven't travelled alone before and wonder what the experience will be like, why not first spend a weekend in another town or city not too far away? Then work up to your fantasy jaunts. Mine include a road trip visiting vintage fairs across the USA, a month living on the French island of Noirmoutier, and a round-the-world trip visiting friends, wherever they may be. Or Italy might seduce me once again. (If countries had a Tinder profile, I'd swipe right for Italy in a flash.)

I like to stretch the holiday vibe as long as possible (pre and post) and enjoy an extensive and meticulous research phase. I love comparing different countries, cities, travel and accommodation options, tourist attractions, restaurants, markets, shopping opportunities and so on. There is nothing I enjoy more than an afternoon of cross-referencing TripAdvisor with blogs and other travel articles, weeding out the paid reviewers and assessing any response to a negative review. The occasional bad review does not deter me, but an overly defensive or poorly judged reply from hotel management can. In a couple of cases I have contacted a manager and got a great deal from them directly.

'The man who goes alone can start today; but he who travels with another must wait till that other is ready, and it may be a long time before they get off.'

HENRY DAVID THOREAU

To set the scene I google 'insider tips' or 'local tips' for my destination, read books and watch movies set there and learn a sprinkling of the language – even a few words can make a huge difference to the welcome you receive. I've been upgraded to nicer rooms, been told about hidden restaurants only known to locals, and even been invited to people's homes because I've fumbled my way through a few sentences with my dodgy accent. Have a look at busuu.com, duolingo. com or rosettastone.eu for language courses, or find Fodor's free online 'Language for Travellers' course, which has 150 key words and phrases you can listen to and repeat.

Save time and avoid the queues when you arrive by booking tickets for major attractions in advance. When it comes to tourist crowds, I'm with Jean-Paul Sartre: 'Hell is other people.' Of course, some people prefer not to research at all and swear by winging it and take advantage of serendipity. I think there's a happy medium. Prepare, research, book, then let yourself go with the flow and be flexible.

I plan my holiday itineraries on a blank monthly calendar, filling each square with flight and accommodation details and daily activities – and those activities are blissfully up to me. You could base a whole holiday around an interest like cooking, snorkelling, photography, art or hiking, or just dip in and out of those worlds for a day… learn how to make pasta in Rome, join an architecture walk in Chicago, or fly a kestrel in Dubai.

The first thing to lock in is your flights. Depending on the flexibility of your dates, you could wait for airline sales (sign up to their alerts) and get good deals by adding more stops. Check out routehappy.com. (And if you are really, really into research, check out the inflight meal reviews at inflightfeed.com.)

I like to have all my accommodation booked in advance and, even if you don't, you'll need at least the first night organised. Research hotels versus Airbnb and all the alternatives in-between at your destination. Your choice of hotel and location are really critical when you are travelling alone, so spend time researching and make it as good as you can afford (although it's worth remembering that you will meet more people at hostel-type accommodation). Single supplements are the bane of the solo traveller's life and we pretty much always pay as much as a couple. Occasionally older hotels will have single rooms tucked away in their armpits, but they are still more than half the price of a double. Ho hum. It's always worth asking politely if they'll consider reducing the price as you're alone, especially if it's off-season and the room wouldn't be occupied anyway. But don't bet the farm on it.

Your holiday dates will obviously have an impact on the cost of your trip. Aim for 'shoulder' periods between high and low seasons, when you'll still have good weather and the tourist sites will be open but with fewer crowds. High seasons are expensive, crowded and coincide with school holidays. Bad, bad, bad. Low seasons are cheaper, but the weather can be dodgy. Having said that I've had some of my happiest times in rural France in the middle of winter, when an out-of-season tourist is treated like an exotic bird that flew off course, or stalking around Venice in the winter fog, or skating the frozen canals with the locals of Amsterdam.

A few practicalities... Make sure you have any injections you need; organise the best travel insurance you can afford; scan or photocopy the key page of your passport (and the cards in your wallet) and leave them at home, with another copy tucked into your suitcase. Buy a timer switch to turn the lights on and off at home while you're away, redirect the mail and ask a neighbour to collect any flyers from your door, so they don't stack up. Put a sticky label with your name, address, email address and phone number inside your suitcase so that it can be identified if it gets lost. Enter passport expiry dates in your diary to ensure you don't get caught out. I have a special travel wallet where I keep my passport, e-ticket, boarding passes and currency. I also make myself an easy 'currency convertor' on a small piece of card ('1 Euro = $A1.50, 5 Euros = $A7.30' etc) and pop it in my wallet.

As for packing, I start writing a list in a notebook a couple of weeks before I go, and then gradually toss those things into my suitcase. This includes all the recharging cords I'll need and an electrical socket convertor. Your sponge bag should contain anti-diarrhoea and constipation pills (to avoid the embarrassment of having to mime your condition at the non English-speaking chemist), headache pills, antiseptic cream, sun cream, anti-mozzie and mozzie bite cream, bandaids, plus any prescription medications you need. I write a list of tops, bottoms, undies, swimming costumes, nighties, jewellery, shoes and so on, and in my head I go through what goes with what and which activities I'll be doing. I tend to over pack, so I've now

'The woman who follows the crowd will usually go no further than the crowd. The woman who walks alone is likely to find herself in places no one has ever been before.'

ALBERT EINSTEIN

learned to take out the 'just in case' pairs of trousers and shoes. Frankly, as you're alone, no one will notice if you're wearing the same thing every day. Leave room for shopping or take an empty squashy bag, but keep an eye on your baggage allowance – if you go over, you are charged by the kilo, and it can get very expensive very quickly.

In my hand luggage I take audiobooks on my phone, a blissful superfine merino wool scarf, my own version of a business class toiletries bag (with eye mask, mini flannel, socks, hand sanitiser, mini deodorant, a sample of Jo Malone perfume and moisturiser), an empty water bottle (to fill up the other side of customs) and a magazine or iPad loaded up with things to watch (noise-cancelling ear buds are top of my wish list).

Seize the day

I have an itinerary of possible (pre-researched) activities listed for each day of the holiday, but if I get sidetracked, so much the better. I have long since lost the compulsion to tick off every well-known sight in town, and find much more joy in the small, unexpected corners and 'B' list (minor) museums. For example, reconstructed within Rome's

---

✳

'It is by studying little things that we attain the great art of having as little misery and as much happiness as possible.'

SAMUEL JOHNSON

sublime, but lesser visited, Museo Nazionale Romano are the vivid 'blue sky and orange tree' frescoes from Claudius's mother Livia's villa. Incredible. You will see what she saw.

Solo travel = guilt-free travel. So let's say, quite theoretically you understand, that if you were in Rome and there was a long queue for St Peter's Basilica, you could decide to give it a miss completely and instead follow your nose down the Via Tunisi to the huge underground Andrea Doria food market to track down the world's best porchetta. Add a bag of mini mozzarella balls, a warm panino, some tomatoes split by the sun and a bunch of basil. Find a bench, settle yourself down and devour a picnic fit for a queen. There should be not even a glimmer of guilt for the unseen treasures of St Peter's. Absolutely none. Licking the tomato juice off your fingers is just as much a taste of real Italy as Michelangelo's Pietà.

I like to seize the very first part of the day and go for an early walk before most people are up. If the loneliness bug is going to bite me, it does so in the evenings, so I might have a leisurely restaurant lunch, an early bite for supper and retire to my hotel room to enjoy a glass of wine in a bubble bath, followed by a book or laptop movie and to plan the day ahead. Or I will discover my favourite restaurant and keep returning night after night: it becomes my 'local'. It's amazing how much friendlier restaurant staff are when they see that you have been back several times (especially if you ask for a recipe!) and it's something you might be less able to do with a travelling companion, who would probably like to try different places.

If you miss having someone to share the experience with, write down your impressions of the day in a notebook as you go along or a journal at the end of the day. It doesn't have to be Shakespeare, or even whole sentences: it's just to capture your thoughts and feelings, and to rekindle them once you're home. You are sharing them with the book. By the same principle, I also take a tiny portable tin of watercolour paints to sketch a couple of scenes on postcard-sized paper – the view from my hotel window, perhaps. I find that just the process of drawing and painting makes me really *look*, and even my silly little daubs are a potent reminder of time and place. I also collect ticket stubs, a CD of local music, a pack of local playing cards, some of the region's cooking utensils and a recipe book, the label from the local beer, business cards from shops and restaurants and I record street sounds on my phone. These all make wonderful memories and I usually make a collage to frame. I prefer this to updating Facebook every few days and, besides, I don't want the world to know I'm not at home.

Of course, you never really travel alone: you are always surrounded by people. It's your choice whether to interact with them or not. Sometimes I do and sometimes I don't. How do you go about meeting people if you want to? There are so many ways – you can meet them on the plane, at a hostel, a class, through Meetup.com, go on a tour, hang out in the hotel lounge or lobby, chat to the diners at the next table in a restaurant or, even easier, at a communal table. If you have the good fortune to find yourself in Paris at the irrepressible Bouillon Chartier restaurant, you'll be seated at a table with others and guaranteed to strike up a conversation. Or at the blissful rooftop terrace of Rome's Hotel Campo de' Fiori, where residents gather in the evening to watch the sun set behind the dome of St Peter's and the conversation flows along with the Prosecco. Or just stay at the same hotel or B&B for a week and you'll get chatting.

You can travel alone without travelling alone by joining a holiday tour. These might be orientated around food and wine, art, or history, and some are aimed at solo travellers. Alternatively – this is something I have never experienced first hand – you might try a cruise. (You either love them or hate them.)

Check online if there is an organisation of local 'greeters' who are happy to share the love of their home city with tourists. Again, if you are in the same place for a few days, go to the same café or market stall and strike up a conversation with the stallholder or wait staff. Think about doing an evening food tour. I did a fantastic tour in the Trastevere area of Rome: we visited a dozen food shops, restaurants and wine bars that I would never have found on my own and it was fun to share perspectives of the city with fellow travellers. If you want something to do in the evening, read blogs, ask locals and keep an eye out for posters advertising events. Some of my favourite evenings came about through serendipitous posters – one was for a recording of internet storytelling event 'The Moth' in a bar in New York. I made friends with people in the queue (an Aussie accent comes in handy sometimes!) and had a great time. Another was a free classical concert in a Prague church.

'I see my path but I don't know where it leads. Not knowing where I am going is what inspires me to travel it.'

ROSALIA DE CASTRO

And, while I'm not a huge sports fan at home, going to a game is a great way to soak up the local atmosphere and get chatting to the people next to you. Check in advance and find yourself rooting for the local basketball or football team... or even sumo wrestlers, as I did in Japan.

Most people are kind. Be open, curious, respectful and enthusiastic towards the prevailing culture and you will be rewarded. Use your travels as an opportunity to move towards something, not away from it. Surprising things can happen: after being date-less in Sydney for an age, I was asked on a date by Maurizio, my taxi driver, within 20 minutes of arriving in Rome. (But that's a story for another time...)

I consider that people take too many photographs when they travel. Don't snap them as a substitute for really looking and taking in the scene. Make your eyes your camera shutter: blink and store the image in your memory. Of course, carefully selected photos are still an important part of the trip and here are a few tips I have picked up:

---- * ----

'I'm not afraid of storms, for I'm learning to sail my ship.'
LOUISA MAY ALCOTT

- Do your homework on how to operate your camera at home and experiment in your own neighbourhood.
- Take pictures of the people you meet. We're often so busy taking pictures of the view that we forget to snap the people who make the trip memorable.
- Take pictures of your feet or your shadow from a similar angle but in different locations – on cobbles, in the water, on grass.
- I love taking pictures of old windows, decorative doors and peeling paint. They look great as a series, with their beautiful faded, muted tones.
- You might find that the same colours keep cropping up. Search them out in clothes, food and architecture. They will make a great composition for a collage when you get home.
- Work out what should and shouldn't be in the frame. Adopt a stylist's eye for crop and angle. Follow the rule of thirds: a basic guideline for composition.
- Get up early and stay up late. The best light is one hour after sunrise and one hour before sunset.
- Take your time – a snapshot doesn't have to be a 'snap', but it can still look spontaneous. The beauty of digital is that you can check everything and go back and correct it straight away.
- Edit ruthlessly as you go along, before you download your photos. It makes for a stronger 'story' and you know you won't do it when you get home.
- Don't store your photos away. I print out the best ones as soon as I get back for my kitchen pinboard or for a collage.

Coming home

For me, one of the most trying aspects of being by myself is never being met at the airport. As everyone around me is being hugged and kissed, it gets to me. So, if you arrive at a reasonable hour, ask a friend to pick you up – I ask my friends to give me that as my birthday present!

Mini breaks

If you are not in a position to afford an overseas holiday, treat yourself to a weekend away, perhaps arranging it around a course or exhibition, to give it purpose and meaning. And if a mini break isn't possible – be imaginative! Theme a day or evening for yourself at home with some appropriate entertainment and food – try feasting on the excellent Danish TV series *Borgen*, while dining on frikadeller meatballs and pickled cucumber.

'Curiosity is, in great and generous minds,
the first passion and the last.'

SAMUEL JOHNSON

Christmas Day

Four of the saddest words in the English language must be 'Christmas dinner for one'. Sounds like an edible suicide note, doesn't it? There is no doubt that Christmas is one of the most challenging times of year to be alone. Suddenly your independent I'mfinebymyselfthankyouverymuch flag that has been flying fiercely hangs a bit limp. Of course you can spend the day very happily with friends or relatives, if that's what you want to do or have as an option. If it's not, try re-framing the day.

I have spent the last seven Christmases alone. It has taken a while to find the formula that works for me, but finally I have cracked it. Post divorce, the children spend the day with my ex and his extended family (I have none). That was confronting to begin with. Initially, kind friends scooped me up and jointed me into their family celebrations. It was very well meant, but made me feel even more isolated to witness someone else's happy family celebration while sitting on the 'waifs and strays' table. All I wanted was what they had. It made me feel I had failed.

Now I choose to be alone. It's only one day and it's a day I plan carefully, creating my own traditions. I think of it as a concentrated holiday for *me*. In October I put a note in my diary to start making Christmas cards. I try to send out a lot of early Christmas cards (or emails) to connect, but also to increase my chances of receiving some! It's a lovely way to know that others are thinking of you, even if it took a prompt! I decorate the tree with the same decorations year after year. (I have a weakness for pale pastel, vintage glass Christmas baubles, which I collect on eBay throughout the year.) I play Christmas songs in the preceding weeks to get me in the mood – my favourites are 'Gaudete',

'A Spaceman Came Travelling', 'Stop the Cavalry' and 'The Coventry Carol'. I buy presents for myself (Tiffany diary, cookbook, Badedas bubble bath, a magazine, maybe some personalised jewellery from Etsy), wrap them up and put them under the tree.

I have established a Christmas Day routine. I wake up early, meditate, then go for a swim – it's Sydney summer! If that's not possible for you, go for a walk: just something to connect with nature. Then I read a good book or magazine I've been saving up and nibble on my favourite foods – a couple of wafer thin slices of Spanish jamón ibérico, some cheese, a white nectarine and a glass of champagne. (Going to church isn't part of my routine, but it might be yours.) I will have lined up a movie or TV series that I want to watch and, if we have organised it ahead of time, a Skype call to friends overseas. (Whatever you do, don't look at Facebook – the endless procession of happy families is overwhelming.) I have a candlelit bath, whatever time of day. I write in my journal too, planning the year ahead. Christmas Day is now a happy, peaceful, low-expectation, mini holiday. Enjoy your own bliss. There is something quite liberating about it. Indeed, some friends are quite jealous of my day, avoiding those family tensions that tend to rise, unbidden, to the surface at this time of year. It has taken me a while to get here, but I have Christmas Day sorted.

Another good option is to spend the day volunteering with a charity that feeds the homeless and disadvantaged. Interestingly, these slots are often over-subscribed and you need to sign up early.

New Year's Eve holds similar horrors for me. Enforced jollity is Not My Thing. My advice is to devise a similar plan to your Christmas one, and lay low.

Eating alone

So who knew? It's a real thing, the fear of eating alone, and it's got a name: solomangarephobia. Images of Edward Hopper's 'Nighthawks' flit through my mind. There's no getting around it, no way of disguising it... you are alone, at a table, eating in public. This one took me a long time to master – not days or months, but years. But we solo diners are not as alone as we think. While it may not feel like it, people eating alone represent the fastest growing group of diners. The Australian online booking service Dimmi reports that reservations for one are rising exponentially every year.

On the positive side, you can usually snag a table for one at even the most popular restaurants. Do your research in advance: know where the restaurant is and how you're going to get there. Make a reservation and choose a time before or after peak hour. Seats near an open kitchen are a good choice when you are by yourself: I enjoy watching the chefs move around with the grace and syncopation of dancers. This is often easier to arrange at lunch rather than at dinner; in fact, if you are new to this, eating alone at lunchtime is a less daunting prospect altogether.

'I love to be alone. I never found the companion that was so companionable as solitude.'

HENRY DAVID THOREAU

If there is a bar that also serves food, you can usually squeeze in and have a good view of what is going on. Communal tables are always easier, but it is still a good idea to take props with you. I think a phone dilutes the bold statement made by the solo diner, but a book, magazine or notepad are all acceptable dining companions, and a scarf is useful to save your place if you go to the loo. As eating alone becomes more common, service and attitudes towards single diners are improving. In the meantime, be strong!

When it comes to ordering, I google the menu in advance to see what's on offer. It makes me feel more in control once I'm there. I tend to stay near the top of the menu and choose two starters (served in succession) plus a salad, rather than a starter and a main course, which can often prove too big (and expensive). When I'm alone I try to notice more, eat less. As a bit of a game, deploy all your senses while eating. Look closely at the colours and textures of the food; close your eyes and see if it tastes different. Eavesdrop on conversations and write a short story in your head about the other diners.

'The happiest of all lives is a busy solitude.'

VOLTAIRE

Acceptance of solo diners varies by country. I can't wait to try the world's first restaurant designed for people dining alone: Eenmaal ('One Meal') in Amsterdam. It describes itself as 'the first one person restaurant in the world and an attractive place for temporary disconnection'. Most people who dine there are not single or living by themselves, but just want time alone. It started as a temporary pop-up but has been so popular it has become permanent and now plans to expand internationally. Tokyo's Moomin House Café takes a different approach to lone patrons, who are automatically seated with a stuffed Moomin hippo-like toy for company. Since the 'lonely-friendly' concept went viral, business has boomed. It sounds a trifle desperate to me. I have eaten my solo way across Asia, India and Europe, Moomin free, no problem!

Some restaurateurs find single diners annoying. Their argument goes: we take up a table for two, we don't drink as much (most of their profits come from alcohol) and we don't contribute to the ambience. I wonder what would be their collective noun for solo diners? An 'irritation', I suspect. I have been asked to move table mid-mouthful to accommodate a group of three, and have been shepherded to a table by the loo more times than I care to remember. It's not ideal, and now I don't accept it and neither should you. There are two ways to avoid it. If you are making a reservation online, there is usually a 'comments' section: put your request in there. Secondly, become a regular at a couple of local restaurants. I'll never forget a charming scene in the Café La Palette in Paris, when all the waiters were fussing around a charismatic elderly lady (clearly a regular) and her little white dog, who sat next to her at the table and had his own steak. Tourists were batted aside and she was treated like a queen.

If you need a confidence boost, adopt an alter ego for the evening. 'Suzanne the foodie' or 'Caroline the out of town businesswoman', or just pretend you are writing a restaurant review. Keep a notebook for when you dine out alone and write about your meal as you experience it. Keep the business card and receipt and stick them in a book, or become an expert in one cuisine in your town – a friend has started a 'dumplings over diamonds' Instagram site, where she rates different dumpling houses all over Sydney.

Solo cinema

This is a guilty pleasure, although I am not sure why as cinemas and theatres are not set up to be social anyway. We are required to sit in silence for two hours. Do it with aplomb, taking the opportunity to escape the world, rather than apologetically fiddling with your phone. There is no stigma when you watch cinema's ugly younger sister, television, alone, so why does the thought of being flanked by two empty red velvet seats make us feel awkward? You get to pick what you really want to see (and here, among friends, I can confess to a weakness

'Unknown in Paris, I was lost in the great city, but the feeling of living there alone, taking care of myself without any aid, did not at all depress me. If sometimes I felt lonesome, my usual state of mind was one of calm and great moral satisfaction.'

MARIE CURIE

for *Star Trek* movies), you can eat what you like, don't have to worry about friends talking or checking their phones throughout the film, and you can go at any time of day. There is something really decadent about going to the movies when it's light.

Again, it is quite nice to keep going back to your local cinema and you can usually get a good deal by joining their movie club. I am lucky enough to live near an art house cinema and am on their email alert, so I try to catch something arty, foreign and mind-stretching every few weeks. If you feel awkward buying a ticket for one, book it online; however, I find there are usually plenty of people going alone. Why not keep a movie notebook and critique and rate each film you see? Take tissues if you're prone to crying (as I am) and don't pick a horror film and then go home to an empty house.

PART 2 MAKING THE MOST OF YOUR TIME ALONE

Martha Beck asked her Facebook followers what was the best gift they could give themselves. The most popular answer by far was 'time' and, more specifically, time *alone*. So we solos should feel incredibly lucky that we have in abundance precisely what many people crave: time alone. However, we don't always feel lucky, do we? There are days when the clock seems to defy the laws of physics and time flies by. Then there are others when a lifetime passes, but the clock hands have only nudged minutes, and all you can see is the giant maw of time yawning to be filled. I don't like that feeling, so I'll try to tackle it head on here.

I'm not talking about work. Living alone, it is all too easy to fall into the trap of regularly working at weekends and in the evenings.

You rarely get thanked for it and after a while people will come to expect it from you. By all means work hard and love your job, but working in your own time is not a substitute for living and your job doesn't hug you back.

Instead, use the time to figure out who you are and what you love, and do it.

Living a bigger life

Living alone makes you responsible for using your time productively. A clue lies in the first word: 'living'. You wouldn't be reading this if you didn't want to *live*, rather than just exist. That means pushing yourself a little – into doing things you might find challenging or uncomfortable. It is harder to make the box of your life bigger than it is to live cosily in a smaller one. I want to push the margins of my life outwards; I get the feeling that some of the most interesting things will happen in that space.

The best things in life are often difficult. When something challenges you and forces you to adapt – learning a language, moving cities, trying a new sport – it keeps you on your toes. You know you are alive.

'It is every man's duty to assume the moral responsibility for his own boredom.'

SAMUEL JOHNSON

Start doing things 'for' and 'with' yourself

Years ago I saw a Nike poster of a woman running; the slogan was simply 'My Time'. Now, years later, that captures the way I think about the time I spend alone. My attitude shifts when I think about doing things 'for' myself or 'with' myself, rather than 'by' myself. (A similar light bulb moment occurred when I first heard the accurate phrase 'learning differences' as opposed to 'learning difficulties'.) It's not semantics. If you are facing a high grey wall of aloneness, it is a useful, in fact vital, way to re-frame your state of being.

Don't look sideways

I often had the sneaking feeling that my friends were off doing marvellous things that didn't include me, while I was plodding away doing boring stuff alone, especially on weekends. Maybe they were out on a boat, or trying a new restaurant, or having a picnic on a beach. Of course they weren't. This wasn't fear of missing out (FOMO) – I just thought other people had more interesting lives than me and that was the price I paid for being alone. Quite apart from the fact that comparison is the thief of joy, the reality is that we all have to do the same stuff – clean the car, go to the supermarket, do the ironing, watch cats playing Jenga on the internet. So keep your eyes forward and think about what you are doing, not what others might be doing.

The mixed blessings of technology

I do seriously love you, my laptop, my precious, but I know that too much of you is not good for me. For starters, I am predisposed to indulge in an unholy orgy of Netflix. It is crack cocaine for the need-to-pass-the-time part of me, but battery acid for the soul when taken in excess. Someone even went as far as to call boxed sets 'a diagnostic tool for depression'. I recognise that too much screen time is a time thief – it diminishes me a bit and can make my mood worse.

Social media is a double-edged sword, genuinely connecting us, but also shoving other people's smugness in our faces. You might find some online communities genuinely supportive and interesting, but many are ersatz, soaking up time that would be better spent making connections with real people. I also wonder, as this thoughtful piece by William Deresiewicz argues, if too much interaction with technology dilutes our own perspective on the world:

'Thinking for yourself means finding yourself, finding your own reality. Here's the other problem with Facebook and Twitter and even *The New York Times*. When you expose yourself to those things, especially in the constant way that people do now – older people as well as younger people – you are continuously bombarding yourself with a stream of other people's thoughts. You are marinating yourself in conventional wisdom. In other people's reality: for others, not for yourself. You are creating a cacophony in which it is impossible to hear your own voice, whether it's yourself you're thinking about or anything else. That's what Emerson meant when he said that "he who should inspire and lead his race must be defended from travelling with the souls of other men, from living, breathing, reading, and writing in the daily, time-worn yoke of their opinions." Notice that he uses the word *lead*. Leadership means finding a new direction, not simply putting yourself at the front of the herd that's heading toward the cliff.'

I feel ambivalent about taking photos on my phone too. The sublime Adele nailed it when she snapped at a concert-goer filming her singing:

'Could you stop filming me with that video camera? Because I'm really here in real life, you can enjoy it in real life rather than through your camera. This isn't a DVD, this is a real show.' I've already mentioned my aversion to taking pictures instead of actually looking at things and it's the same with taking photos of your food. They just become part of a virtual stamp collection and lessen the responsibility of your taste buds to enjoy the meal.

Digital detox holidays are enjoying rapid growth and I am not surprised. The Gin Tub, a bar in Hove, England, has enjoyed a surge in popularity since it started blocking mobile phone signals. (Mind you, The Gin Tub sounds like fun anyway!) Just as we are trying to make our nutritional diet healthier, it's worth also thinking about our digital diet, taking care of what we watch and searching out things we can learn from.

Familiar interests...

In the next section we'll think about new things to do, but first, let's look closer to home, at interests you already have. Rather than just turning the topsoil of an existing hobby, how about digging deeper and mining the seams that hold diamonds? Obviously you can pursue

'The intellect must not be kept at consistent tension, but diverted by pastimes ... The mind must have relaxation, and will rise stronger and keener after recreation.'

SENECA

223

The Art of Living Alone & Loving It

interests as a couple, but being alone gives you the opportunity to fling yourself into them passionately, with abandon and absorption. Dance with your curiosity. Flirt with your proclivities. Don't just cast a fishing line, throw in a whole illegal mile-long trawling net! That could mean reading up in detail on a subject, signing up to a course or a series of lectures, or perfecting an existing skill. Rather than tackling a lot of different interests, try to focus deeply on one or two areas, like putting blinkers on a horse.

This is also a huge opportunity to develop professionally. You might consider a course that will enhance your current occupation or hone your digital skills, or tackle something new if you are considering a switch in careers. Lynda.com has a massive range of online courses that you can browse.

... and new inspirations

'A mind stretched by a new idea can never shrink back to its original dimensions.' Oliver Wendell Holmes

If you feel a bit Groundhog Day-ish, and find your daily choreography is being repeated over and over, force yourself to do something new each week. 'Interested' = 'interesting'. 'Furnish your mind' said Helen

———————————————— ✳ ————————————————

'Learning is like rowing upstream; not to advance is to drop back.'
CHINESE PROVERB

Gurley Brown, the legendary feminist and editor of *Cosmopolitan*. If we don't push our minds, they stagnate, so shake things up and make new memories along the way. Here are a few ideas:

- If inspiration doesn't strike, potter about your home and follow the metaphorical trail of breadcrumbs. Little clues will present themselves. Think of this as the prologue to a play. An old book, unfinished craft project, souvenir or photograph might trigger a memory of something you wanted to do but gave up, or inspire you to try something new. The Japanese proverb *On-ko chi-shin* ('Study something old to learn something new') captures this idea well.

- Write a list of all the minor museums in your area and tick them off, one by one.

- Go to an art gallery and allow your gut instinct to choose just two or three paintings to *really* look at. What are they trying to tell you that is relevant to your life right now?

- Become a *flâneuse*. Lauren Elkin describes a *flâneuse* as 'a determined resourceful woman keenly attuned to the creative potential of the city, and the liberating possibilities of a good walk'. She has written a book called *Flâneuse: Women Walk the City in Paris, New York, Tokyo, Venice and London*, which traces the paths of cross-dressing nineteenth century novelist George Sand, Parisian artist Sophie Calle, journalist Martha Gellhorn and writer Jean Rhys. Walk your city with new eyes and map it with your feet.

- Find yourself a new grassy hillside and enjoy a solo picnic.

- Paint or draw a self-portrait. Look at some of Frida Kahlo's for inspiration. She said: 'I am my own muse, I am the subject I know best. The subject I want to know better.'

- Get to know your neighbourhood intimately – learn its best walks and history (take photos of old houses before they are knocked down), try the sport venues, theatre and library. There is often more on offer than you realise.
- Go to a drop-in dance class or learn a dance routine (YouTube!)
- Fly a kite.
- Go on an 'Artist's Date', as recommended in Julia Cameron's bestselling *The Artist's Way*. This is a solo expedition to develop your creative self, 'enchant yourself' and refill your creative inner well so that when you go to fish, there's something swimming there. It could be a trip to an art supply or fabric shop, a garden, art gallery or cinema. She describes the concept at juliacameron.com.
- Draw a mandala.
- Explore your local parks and gulp down some natural wonder.
- The wonder of the internet is the 'long tails' of people who share niche interests, such as photographing 'ghost signs', the faded advertising painted on old commercial buildings. Find one that captures your interest.
- Inspire yourself with a TED talk.
- Learn to meditate with Headspace.
- Find a podcast series you love. (ABC radio's *Conversations* with Richard Fidler is a good place to start.)
- I am also a sucker for spoken-word radio, especially BBC Radio 4 dramas (*15 Minute Drama*, *Afternoon Drama* and *Book at Bedtime* are firm favourites).
- Browse Pinterest and make up some dream boards.
- Go to Meetup.com and find a like-minded group to do things with.
- Write the outline of your life story.

- Draw your childhood home – the view from the outside and the layout – making note of any special memories the rooms spark in you.
- Do a first-aid course.
- Give blood.
- Volunteer for a charity (try govolunteer.com.au).
- Learn something from the French Whisperer on YouTube. I won't spoil your fun by telling you what to expect.
- Learn the planets in the solar system. There's an app for it!
- Learn a poem. Start with the anthology *Poems that make Grown Women Cry* edited by Anthony and Ben Holden. (T.S. Eliot described poetry as 'writing with a lot of silence on the page.')

Sometimes to find where the edge is you have to put your toes over it, so reach out.

'Do not be too timid and squeamish about your
actions. All life is an experiment.'

RALPH WALDO EMERSON

Read yourself bigger

Proust wrote, 'We read to know ourselves', which may explain my renewed pleasure in books. Cassandra Clare said, 'One must always be careful of books, and what is inside them, for words have the power to change us'. You're never alone with a book, as Niccolò Machiavelli noted 500 years ago: 'I strip off my muddy, sweaty, workaday clothes, and ... I enter the antique courts of the ancients ... and for the space of four hours I forget the world.' Or, as W.H. Auden pointed out, 'A real book is not one that we read, but one that reads us'. Certainly there are not many other activities that offer us the opportunity to go brain-to-brain with another human being, as we do when reading an author's words. I now read with a highlighter and also note down particular phrases that please me.

Consider joining an online book club, such as the BBC World Service 'World Book Club', which interviews a different author monthly. You can listen to old episodes as podcasts. Check out your local library too. I listen to many more books than I read. At the moment I am tackling six Jane Austens in audiobook as I yomp across the park. Other audiobooks I've enjoyed include *H is for Hawk* by Helen Macdonald, anything by David Sedaris or Bill Bryson and a slew of exceptional BBC

---

*

'Without knowledge, life is no more but the shadow of death.'

MOLIERE

productions – *The Martin Beck Mysteries* by Per Wahlöö and Maj Sjöwall, dramatisations of Dickens and Austen, *A Suitable Boy* by Vikram Seth (recorded in India) and Sherlock Holmes dramatisations.

I find myself more and more particular about what I read, happily ditching a book halfway through if I'm not enjoying it. They say there are two categories of books that you don't finish: those that aren't good enough, and those for which you are not yet good enough. There are 129 million titles in the world – better get cracking!

Self-development

Without wishing to dip a toe into the seductive pool of self-obsession, living alone does offer a unique opportunity to develop as a human being. This whole book is about precisely that, so I'm not going to labour the point, except to say that for years I was embarrassed to be seen in the 'self-help' section of the bookstore. It helped me when they re-named it 'self-enrichment'. After all, you'd be foolish not to want to enrich yourself, wouldn't you? My only note of warning, having-been-there-seen-it-done-it, is that it is easy to buy loads of self-help books, flick through them once, put them on your bookshelf and leave them there. More 'shelf-improvement' than 'self-improvement'. There's nothing more depressing than a bookcase full of them, casting judgement because *The Secret* (law of attraction) didn't work for you, because you don't care who moved your cheese, you're not interested in chicken soup for the soul or because you feel you are the only person in the world who hasn't defined their life purpose.

No one book will answer your questions. So flick through them, pick out the best thoughts, write them in your journal and then give the books away.

Creativity is the child of solitude

There are many great achievers who never married and who lived alone, including Isaac Newton, Fredrich Nietzshe, Beatrix Potter, Emily Dickinson, Greta Garbo and Beethoven.

You might find your creativity blossoming during time spent alone, as it did 100 years ago for Australian artist Clarice Beckett. She had a very domineering father, turned down several offers of marriage, had a couple of lovers, but spent most of her time looking after her ill parents. The only time she escaped her duties was when walking the suburbs of Melbourne at dawn and dusk to paint. Her creativity blossomed in solitude. She died aged 47, unknown until her sister walked into a gallery with a parcel of paintings and sketches 40 years later. This led to the discovery of over 2000 works in an old shed that was open to the elements. Many were damaged beyond repair, but a few have survived. They are beautiful; her sadness and resilience forged them in solitude.

Many people have found Julia Cameron's *The Artist's Way* helpful for accessing their innate creativity (there is now an online course as well as the original book). I always wince a little when I hear 'we are all creative', but it is true. Often it is squashed out of us when we are children. When I was about seven, I wrote a poem about my bedroom. I took care writing it and remember being quite pleased with it, but the teacher gave me a D because she refused to believe I had written it myself. As a consequence, I never wrote another poem. Until last month! I have no doubt I would not have written it were I not living alone. Success is the best form of revenge, so stick two fingers up to the doubters and show them what you can do. Don't just uncover your creativity – unleash it.

Creativity can be applied to many aspects of life – cooking, how you dress, how you decorate your house. I enjoy arty crafty stuff. I don't have the luxury of enough space to keep brushes and paints out all the time, so I have a different canvas bag for each of my projects – Chinese brush paintings of fish, watercolours, an altered book and some embroidery on toile inspired by textile artist Richard Saja are my current projects. I like having a bag to dip into for an hour or two.

Living alone, I am an island, but an interesting island, full of exciting places to explore.

Embrace boredom

My generation was the last to fully experience boredom. Technology now fills the spaces between the stones. Years ago I went to see *The Highlights of the Bolshoi Ballet*. I was very much looking forward to it, but it turned out to be one of the most boring shows I had ever seen, because the highlights (big jumps, twirling around and around a thousand times) lose their power and wonder without the calm, slow parts as contrast. Boredom is no bad thing if it means you can be quiet and listen. Boredom and breakthrough can be twins.

---- ✳ ----

'Boredom transforms into something else. Boredom is the uncomfortable bit and then what you break through to is reverie – those higher planes of creative thought.'

MICHAEL HARRIS, *THE END OF ABSENCE*

However, if it really gets to you, make yourself an anti-boredom kit. Write down suggestions for things to do on slips of paper and put them in a box. They might be practical (tidy out three drawers, clean the fridge) or more creative (learn a poem, call two friends, send a real hand-written letter to a friend you've lost contact with). Dip into your ideas box if you're ever hit by the boredom stick.

Give yourself a break

Literally and metaphorically. Not every day has to be high achieving. I am tired of feeling I need to be capable all the time. It is important to recharge your batteries and refill the well. Give yourself permission to disengage completely now and again. Take a day or evening off and chill out to the max. Make yourself something comforting to eat (my choice is usually Nigel Slater's shepherd's pie), pour a glass of good red wine and watch a movie, perhaps with some pieces of the bitterest, darkest, most expensive chocolate you can lay your hands on.

And don't forget the words of the immortal Willy Wonka: 'A little nonsense now and then is relished by the wisest men.'

TAKE AWAYS

Don't ever be intimidated by
doing something alone.

The more you challenge yourself, the
more confident you will become, standing
up to the curiosity and pity of friends and
family. You are an armadillo!

When travelling, don't look: see;
don't hear: listen; don't learn: understand.
Plan your next solo trip now.

Plan strategies for Christmas, eating alone
and lovely solo cinema excursions.

Do things *with*, or *for* yourself, not *by* yourself.

Plan your digital interactions.

Do familiar things more deeply, or push yourself
to try new things. Just do *something*. The poet
Wallace Stevens called it 'stepping across the line'.

Embrace boredom and give
yourself a break.

If your ship hasn't come in, swim out to it.

Chapter 9

SOLO SPIRITUALITY

Why it is important ✶ *What you are looking for and how to incorporate it into your life* ✶ *Facing up to grief and death*

Spirituality is an intensely personal and complex subject, not just another item to tick off the self-development check list. I am a pragmatist and have already told you about my sensitive bullshit antenna, so it shouldn't come as a surprise that I find much of what has been written about spirituality and religion incomprehensible and confusing. I want to make this subject inspirational and practical for you. Simply, how do you go about finding what works for you and applying it to your life?

Before we set out on this journey of discovery, we need to define what we are looking for. Three questions:

Why is spirituality important?
What do I do to find what I am looking for?
How do I incorporate it into everyday life?

WHY?

Why is it important to have spirituality in your life? What role does it play? You have to be very strong to live alone and having an internal life reinforces you, inside and out. Spirituality has two sides, like Janus, the god with two faces. One side is a well, an internal reservoir of courage and wisdom you can draw on. The other side informs and feeds your energy and the way you project yourself to the world. Once you have found equilibrium between them, you will also be in a much stronger position to help others.

When I asked solo women what prompts them to look deeper, this is what they said:

'I want to explore a different part of my life – it's not my work, or friends, or my home or day to day life. It's a separate part of me. It's very personal.'

'I feel there is a whole part of myself that is unexplored.'

'More *being*, less *doing*.'

'I want to understand myself better.'

'I want to uncover my authentic self.'

'I feel hollow inside.'

'I want to give back.'

'I recently got divorced. I am desperately sad and need to get some perspective.'

'I want some peace.'

'Untangle the ball of wool that is my life and make it simpler.'

'I want to believe in something other than myself.'

'I feel disconnected from myself.'

'My mother's death has made me rethink everything.'

'I want to calm my monkey mind.'

'I feel I am just beginning to wake up.'

'I feel incomplete.'

'It's part of my transformation.'

'I want to find a way to integrate something spiritual into my day to day life.'

'I don't feel religious, but feel there is something bigger than me.'

'I see an energy in some of my friends that I would like to have too.'

'I am scared of dying.'

'I just want to learn to meditate.'

'I feel a sort of spiritual itch that needs to be scratched.'

'I want to unearth my purpose.'

Our advantage

Identifying what spirituality means to us individually, what works, and how to incorporate it into our lives, requires time and space. Fortunately, we soloists are rich in both commodities. This is where we have a distinct advantage and we owe it to ourselves to make the most of it to explore this part of our lives. Solitude makes it easier to connect to the spiritual self, to explore and maintain a connection with the inner world. Your spirituality will unfurl.

WHAT?

This is an adventure of the soul, so rather than pushing yourself to *do*, relax, explore a few different things and see what resonates. Sometimes it takes a while to recognise the path that is right for you and initially it can be confronting. You might not like what you see when, sometimes for the first time in a while, you step back and look within. We don't usually tackle these big questions because they're fun or have easy answers: they can bring us to our knees. This is a journey for the brave.

'The most frequent impediment to men's turning the mind inwards upon themselves is that they are afraid of what they shall find there. There is an aching hollowness in the bosom, a dark, cold speck at the heart, an obscure and boding sense of somewhat, that must be kept out of sight of the conscience; some secret lodger, whom they can neither resolve to eject or retain.' Samuel Taylor Coleridge

So you are not alone in being apprehensive. Don't let it daunt you. Think of it as the foxing on an old mirror falling away to reveal a clear reflection.

The benefits of solitude

History offers up many examples of men and women, who have used solitude to their advantage to better understand themselves and access a higher power. I am not advocating whipping off to a cave for 40 days and 40 nights, but we can maybe take a small leaf out of their book.

A favourite of mine is Saint Jerome, who spent time alone in the desert, along the way removing a thorn from the paw of a passing lion. The lion followed him around like a dog for the rest of his life. I particularly love the painting of Jerome by Antonello da Messina in the National Gallery in London – he is depicted reading in his study, which is set in a beautiful architectural space. I love the atmosphere of concentration and self-containment it exudes (not to mention the beautifully observed details, such as the cat curled at his feet, the towel draped on a hook, and his lion in the shadows). Jerome is utterly self-possessed. And alone.

The joy of silence

'As time passes I increasingly realise that there is an interior dimension to silence, a sort of stillness of heart and mind which is not a void but a rich space,' wrote Sara Maitland in her excellent *A Book of Silence*. She rented a small isolated cottage on the Isle of Skye and waited, and listened to the silence. She discovered much more than she expected, including physical changes, such as an intensifying of her senses of taste and hearing, her sense of body temperature becoming more acute and a concentration of emotions – joy, sadness and giggles. She became disinhibited, only washing once a week but relishing her hot bath – no need to conform to society's norms. She tells of many other people who had similar experiences. And it was not just from being isolated and alone: she felt that the silence itself 'unskinned' her.

The American composer John Cage wrote 4'33" ('Four minutes, thirty-three seconds') of silence. It is a three-movement piece in which the musicians were not allowed to play their instruments – the silence was filled with the ambient sounds the audience could hear, and these became the piece itself. (You can see a performance on YouTube.) It's amazing what you can hear in silence. Try to weave some silence into the fabric of each day. Dawn is a good place to start. I find myself getting up earlier and earlier and love this time of the day – it feels as if a secret

---- ✳ ----

'And you, when will you begin that long journey into yourself?'

RUMI

I have to myself. Anthony Robbins calls this 'the hour of power' and Hal Elrod made a 'thing' out of it with his book *Miracle Morning*, which is worth a look.

Listen to your intuition

'Always trust your instincts' is something I believe so strongly that I had it printed at the bottom of every page of my book *Midlife Manifesto*. But maybe it is *intuition* rather than instincts that we should pay attention to? What's the difference between the two? You don't have a conscious choice about instinct. It is hardwired and will cause you to respond in a certain way, whether you like it or not. The knowledge is set in the hollow of your bones, like raising your hands if someone is about to hit you, or jumping at a loud noise. Intuition is more of a feeling or a hunch that makes one way of reacting more attractive than another, but you are still free to choose whether to follow it or not. It is informed by your experiences. The quieter you are, the louder the voice of intuition, your spiritual GPS. Listen to it and it will lead you towards a spiritual perspective and practice that is right for you.

As Lisa Kogan said, 'Yes, spiritual enlightenment and sandals are good. But so are air-conditioning and indoor plumbing. You can find spiritual enlightenment wherever you are, whenever you're ready.'

Make your own rules

We forget that the world's greatest spiritual leaders were the firebrands and radicals of their day, exhorting their followers not to accept blindly what had gone before. By making an effort to understand and question the past, and find the parts that resonate, we are honouring the path laid out by those great minds. They challenged aspects of dogma that might have been relevant centuries earlier. Even Buddha on his deathbed told his disciples: 'Do not accept what you hear by report, do not accept tradition, do not accept a statement because it is found in our books, nor because it is in accord with your belief, nor because it is the saying of your teacher. Be lamps unto yourselves.'

We all want to experience what the American mythologist Joseph Campbell called 'the rapture of being alive'. There is no one path. Each of us is a sentient being with our own mind. What is right for me might not be right for you. 'Religions are like cookbooks and guidebooks: they are not the food or the foreign country; rather they suggest ingredients and point us in the right direction,' writes Elizabeth Lesser in *The Seeker's Guide* (which I highly recommend). You are the only one who can plot your journey.

Start with an open mind

By the time you reach the point in your life where you are curious about exploring spirituality, you might have acquired a few rusted-on opinions, like barnacles on a whale. These could include your existing religious or spiritual beliefs, or those of your parents or friends. While that is not necessarily a bad thing, it is always worth taking a step back to look with fresh eyes.

I am fortunate to live in a part of the world and in an era when questioning accepted wisdom, and even the existence of God, does not result in being ducked in the village pond. We are free to consider all sides of the debate. It is fascinating when you hear someone as articulate as Stephen Fry putting forward a very compelling anti-God argument. Have a look at the YouTube interview: Stephen Fry on God/The Meaning of Life. He doesn't pull any punches. For example, when asked what he'd say to God at the pearly gates, he replied, 'Bone cancer in children? What's that about? How dare you. How dare you create a world where there is such misery that is not our fault. It's not right. It is utterly, utterly evil. Why should I respect a capricious, mean minded, stupid god who creates a world which is so full of injustice and pain?' My father would have agreed with him. He lost his faith after the Second World War, when he simply could not reconcile a god who let six million of his chosen people die in the Holocaust.

There is no doubt that organised religion can offer those who live by themselves spiritual sustenance, as well as a good way to connect with other like-minded people and belong to a 'tribe' or congregation. There are so many different faiths and practices; it is worth learning more if you are curious. Consider doing a short course on comparative religion and even attend different religious services (obviously asking respectful permission when necessary). I have been to services in a mosque, a synagogue and a Russian orthodox church, but found a Quaker meeting the most moving. Sometimes attending a service from a different faith can act as a circuit breaker, making you question your preconceptions and beliefs and helping refine your individual approach to spirituality, like whittling a stick. Go to your local library and pull out books on religions, mythology, philosophy and psychology that pique your interest.

Open your chest wide. Put your hand in the middle where your ribs join. Some spiritual traditions call this the 'heart centre'. Open it up to new thoughts.

What's your spiritual 'fastpass'?

Disney has a 'fastpass' ticketing system in their theme parks, offering a shortcut to the front of the queue. Keep an eye out for things that can do the same in your spiritual life, allowing you faster access to deeper spiritual waters. A mantra, for example, or a crystal, an image, a statue, Mala beads, a bangle or even the physical space where you regularly meditate or worship. One friend has a tattoo inside her wrist that helps her focus. Some people who are highly attuned can feel the patina of devotion when they enter certain places of worship, such as a temple or church.

Walking a labyrinth has the same effect. I recently tried this for the first time here in Sydney, in the company of about a dozen women (none of whom I had met before), under the gentle guidance of American spiritualist Judith Tripp. It was a sort of gentle walking meditation. We started sitting down and meditated for a short time,

'When you do something from your soul,
you feel a river moving in you, a joy.'

RUMI

before standing up in a circle and holding hands. Judith asked us to think about our families, our ancestors and other women in the world all standing behind us, supporting us. She told us to think of our feet as roots connecting us to nature and the centre of the earth, and imagine the branches of trees putting their arms about us, embracing us. At this point some of you will be googling 'Where's the nearest labyrinth?' and others will have flung this book across the room. Labyrinth walking may not be for everyone, but the point is to try new things. Trail your fingers through the water.

As Marianne Williamson beautifully put it: 'Wisdom is like a marinade. First you take what a book said, or what a teacher said, and then you mix it with your own ideas. Then you add experiences and pour in a few buckets of tears. Add memories of lost love, a pinch of personal humiliation and a teaspoon of deep regrets. Add to that a cup of courage. Leave it to soak for a few years and – voila – darn it if you have not become wise.'

Spending time in nature is another spiritual 'fastpass' for me, and I can see why the Japanese 'forest bathing' or *shinrin-yoku* (basically being in the presence of trees) has been proven to lower heart rate and blood pressure, reduce stress hormone production, boost the immune system and improve overall feelings of wellbeing.

'There can be no very black melancholy to him who lives in the midst of Nature and has his senses still ... I have never felt lonesome, or in the least oppressed by a sense of solitude.'

HENRY DAVID THOREAU

Here are a few quick ways to connect with nature:

- Lie on your back and watch the stars.
- Put your bare feet on grass.
- Savour the weather. Walk in the rain and get your face wet.
- Enjoy the changing seasons.
- Watch out for birds.
- Bring nature into your home. Rather than flowers, put branches in a big vase, a collection of driftwood or some abandoned nests and feathers.
- Listen to the sea breathe – or just a recording of it.
- Choose a bird or animal you identify with as your 'spirit guide' for a day. Get some lovely old books of animal prints from a second-hand shop as inspiration.
- Find some art that repays contemplation. Some of my favourties are Monet's Water Lilies from the Musée de l'Orangerie in Paris, Rothko's Seagram paintings, Antony Gormley's haunting installation 'Another Place' and his 'Angel of the North', Elisabeth Frink sculptures… oh the list goes on.

Alternatively, find your patron saint or even align yourself to an ancient goddess to help access your spiritual self. When I set out to write this book, I hoped to find the Patron Saint of People Living Alone. After all, beltmakers, comedians, Italian prison officers and even STDs have patron saints (Saint Alexius, Saint Genesius, Saint Basilides and Saint Fiacre respectively). So why not us? Sadly, I was disappointed. Maybe we can appropriate one. (Wikipedia has a list of patron saints handily indexed by occupation and activity.)

To find a 'patron' ancient goddess whose characteristics are in line with yours, go to goddessmeca.com (or google 'find goddess archetype') and do the quiz. I was most like the goddess Hekate, and I felt the feedback was pretty accurate for me: 'If this is your archetype you are capable of living in the present and trusting the universe. Career choices could span the arts, telecommunications, motivational speaker or life coach. You know the world's illusionary and you value spiritual connection. Oprah Winfrey is a perfect example of this archetype. This is a powerful archetype for the woman who is capable of ageing in an interesting and healthy manner. If this is your archetype you have the gift of seeing life as a series of lessons and have probably developed a great sense of humour. Life is viewed as a rich tapestry, beautiful despite its inherent flaws.'

Why not give it a crack, to add a different perspective?

Charlatans and crackpots?

In case you are now thinking I have completely lost the plot, I am not purporting that ancient goddesses are The Answer. But they might be another piece of the jigsaw puzzle, another bead on our spiritual necklaces. For the record, I have seen tarot and oracle card readers, made multiple visits to a psychic, seen someone who says they can converse with the dead, and I own a beautiful set of Lenormand tarot cards. Am I 100 per cent convinced of their usefulness, accuracy and insight? No. Do I think they are a complete waste of time and money, utter bullshit and the provenance of hustlers? No. The jury's out. For me, the truth lies somewhere in between.

What I can report is that each time I have seen one of these people I had a specific issue in mind and by the end of the session it was resolved in some way. I accept that this might be my post-rationalising to justify the visit, but if it made me feel better, then it's a success as far as I am concerned. Some friends have found that oracle cards in particular can be helpful when making a decision or setting the course for the day. For the investment of a few dollars, why not try them out? I bought a pack of 'Goddess Inspiration Oracle' cards by Kris Waldherr, but Doreen Virtue is the best-known 'queen' of the oracle cards, focusing primarily on angels.

Of course we are responsible for our own futures and we can't subcontract that job to oracle cards and psychics, but if they help give us clarity of thought or a nudge in the right direction, in my mind that's a good thing.

Bullshit-free meditation and mindfulness

Buddhists say that we can learn everything we need to know about the world by sitting on a cushion. But that's easier said than done. The writers of an experiment in *Science* magazine in 2014 found that participants typically did not enjoy spending even six to 15 minutes in a room alone, with nothing to do but think. They enjoyed doing mundane activities and many *preferred to administer electric shocks to themselves* rather than being left alone with their thoughts. The paper concludes: 'Most people seem to prefer to be doing something rather than nothing, even if that something is negative.' I find that incredible, but I also understand that the benefits of sitting quietly and doing nothing take a while to reveal themselves. I have finally learned that if you lie in a river of stillness, the eddies and currents will actually take you places. It is the adventure of going nowhere.

I needed no encouragement to try meditation and there many scientific studies that prove its value. However, I am still meditating on L-plates and I have to keep telling myself that the more I do it the easier and more beneficial it will become. Just 10 minutes at the same time every day, Jane. How hard can that be? We set ourselves such a high expectation of what meditation can deliver that it is almost off-putting, especially if we don't experience remarkable change immediately. If you are starting out, think of meditation as just the practice of being alone and being comfortable with it. Less of the 'to do' and more of the 'to be'.

Elizabeth Lesser writes that meditation is used 'to pierce the veil between our ordinary consciousness and the "angelic realms"'. I have yet to achieve any moments of bliss or reach those elusive 'angelic realms' myself. However, even if meditation is just your mind's way of 'deleting the trash', like you do on a computer, then it's worth it. The author Ken Robinson describes it as 'a powerful way of reconnecting with yourself and brightening your sense of who you are beneath the surface'. And, yes, it's not called a 'meditation *practice*' for nothing. Practise makes permanent.

Having a teacher will keep you on track, but you can learn how to meditate on your own. There are many different disciplines, but the basic principles are similar, with the focus on the breath and letting thoughts come and then float away. It's not about knocking thoughts on the head, but about calming the busy, so-called 'monkey mind'. (A misnomer, as it turns out monkeys are very focused!) I have found the app Headspace to be most helpful in getting me started and keeping me on track. The English narrator, Andy, walks you through the practice in a clear and straightforward way. It is an excellent place both to start and continue your meditation journey.

'Our life is an endless journey; it is like a broad highway that extends infinitely into the distance. The practice of meditation provides a vehicle to travel on that road. Our journey consists of constant ups and downs, hope and fear, but it is a good journey. The practice of meditation allows us to experience all the textures of the roadway, which is what the journey is all about.' Chögyam Trungpa

Sometimes, for variety, I practise Vietnamese Zen Buddhist monk Thích Nhat Hanh's Four Pebbles meditation. It was originally designed for children, so it's nice and simple. Find four smooth pebbles (or polished stones from a crystal shop) that appeal to you, and assign each one a role and quality. The first one is a flower to represent freshness, the second a mountain for solidity, the third, still water for calm and tranquility and the last stone is space for freedom. These four aspects – freshness, solidity, calm and freedom – form the basis of the meditation.

--------------------------------- ✳ ---------------------------------

'We can develop our minds infinitely – there is no limitation. Many of us are discontent with how many possessions we have, but we're content when it comes to our spiritual development. That is the first mistake we make.'

TENZIN GYASTO, 14TH DALAI LAMA

Once you have settled, hold each stone in your hands, one by one, and focus on the quality it represents. As you breathe in and out, think of the image and the quality:

- The first pebble, breathing in 'I feel fresh' and out 'I am a flower'.
- The second pebble, breathing in 'I am solid' and out 'I am a mountain'.
- The third pebble, breathing in 'water, stillness' and out 'reflecting'.
- The fourth pebble, breathing in 'I feel space inside me and around' and out 'I am free'.

There is (of course!) a YouTube video to guide you – Pebble Pocket Meditation. I keep my stones in a little bag on my mini 'altar' with a card to remind me which stone is which.

I still find it hard to get my head around mindfulness, meditation's slightly try-hard younger brother. Mindfulness has been described as 'non judgemental awareness' of the moment we are in, pausing the commentary in our heads. Thích Nhat Hanh teaches that this moment is the only one we have complete control over, so is therefore the most important thing in our life. We need to stop always thinking that there's something better round the corner and just enjoy what we are doing right now. For me, the most practical way of incorporating mindfulness into my life is to press the pause button for a moment, savour and appreciate some of the mundane things I do, as if it were for the first or the last time, even if that is just eating an apple. Watch a very good interview between Oprah and Thích Nhat Hanh on the subject of mindfulness online.

Define your version of spirituality

'One is not born a woman, one becomes one,' said Simone de Beauvoir. Living alone and embracing our spiritual side concentrates the process of growth. It is an important part of our maturing as human beings and sentient souls.

How, or if, you choose to formally define your version of spirituality is up to you. I find it helpful to think of it like a necklace, composed of a bead here (e.g. meditation) and a bead there (e.g. labyrinth). Mine is still in its early days although I think it is making progress when I find myself being more patient and forgiving, meditating when standing in a queue or appreciating the impact of nature. It's a good feeling and it seems to be gaining traction.

Oprah coined it well when she mused that it isn't until you come to a spiritual understanding of who you are (which might not be a religious feeling, but the spirit deep within you) that you finally begin to take control.

HOW?

How do you incorporate spirituality into your daily life? I think it often manifests itself as attitude. An attitude that defines how you approach life and the different situations you encounter. It informs everything you do; it is your guard rail. Hopefully you will feel happier and more peaceful because you have what you need to be fulfilled inside yourself, or at least know where to look for inspiration and guidance. You don't need anyone else. Pay attention to, and cultivate, your inner life. Become a scholar of self and soul. Expose yourself to different aspects of spirituality and religion, and then succumb to your intuition. Get the *being* right and the *living* will follow.

'When I do good, I feel good. When I do bad, I feel bad. That is my religion,' said Abraham Lincoln. If we act the same way over and over again, it eventually becomes the way we are.

I try to shy away from frenemies who pull me down, and avoid materialism, rudeness, busyness and gossip. I aim to direct myself towards curiosity, open-mindedness and finding the best in other people and in myself. You can live your life in the shallow end or in the deep end. It's easier to make splashes in the shallow end; the deep is much more rewarding, but it does take more work.

It is a good idea to have some sort of physical reminder of spirituality in your home. It could be a quiet place to sit, a special picture or a collection of objects. I have an eclectic grouping of religious items on a desk in my bedroom. Small wooden gilded Italian triptychs and diptychs featuring Catholic saints rub shoulders with a carved wooden Buddha with beads round his neck, and a small brass Hindu Singhasan (throne) with a tiny Ganesh on it. I love the look of this beautiful and calming tableau and for some reason I feel it offers me protection.

The whole subject of spirituality is an incredibly personal one and well suited to us soloists. Elizabeth Cady Stanton captured it well. 'Our inner being which we call ourself, no eye nor touch of man or angel has ever pierced.'

If you are feeling a bit lost or overwhelmed, give yourself a day's sabbatical. Take time to rest and think and listen to your inner self. Most of the answers to the questions we have already lie within us. Your wings may feel a little broken and ruffled, but wrap them lovingly around yourself and relax.

Once you have found some sort of inner equilibrium you might discover that synchronicity starts making its presence felt. That is a marvellous feeling, and much more than mere coincidence. It could be that the person you have been thinking about calls you out of the blue, or a book you have been looking for is on the top of the pile in the second-hand bookshop, or you meet someone who is an expert in a subject you have just become interested in. When I am 'shut down' spiritually, synchronicity dries up. When I am open, confident and optimistic (even if I'm role playing to get there!) it starts happening.

In *On My Own* Florence Falk writes of 'self-blessing' as a final stage before stepping out. I think that is a lovely idea. A bit of a positive acknowledgement that you are on your own spiritual path. Your private Camino Way.

GRIEF AND DEATH

I think it is important to touch on the subject of death in this book: living alone is not about flinching. I will approach this topic in two ways. The first is the experience of grief when someone close to you dies, and the second is the contemplation of our own death.

Grief

I still can't truly believe my parents are dead. That happens to other people, not to the two people I loved best in the world, who knew me inside out, whose hands and turns of phrase I knew, who I could be completely relaxed with. Parents' deaths mark the true beginning of adulthood, when we realise we are the next cab off the rank, but the death of anyone close to us (or even a celebrity) rattles us. Everyone feels and expresses their grief in their own way, and that is how it should be. A part of me rather admires the *sang froid* of the English (epitomised by the royal family at Diana's funeral) and I loathe the mawkish crosses, teddy bears and plastic flowers attached to trees and telegraph poles as memorials for accidents. But there is another primal part of me that, when my parents died, wanted to behave like Boudicca, queen of the Iceni – cover myself in woad and scream and scream.

Part of that screaming is because we look back and miss them and part is in reminder of our own tentative grip on life as we look forward. It is a tap on the shoulder.

The passage below captures the feelings of grief beautifully and I don't think I can better it. I came across it online and can't find the name of the writer, but I reproduce it here with my acknowledgement and thanks. It appeared in response to someone who simply wrote:

'My friend just died. I don't know what to do.'

This was the reply:
'All right, here goes. I'm old. What that means is that I've survived (so far) and a lot of people I've known and loved did not. I've lost friends, best friends, acquaintances, co-workers, grandparents, mom, relatives, teachers, mentors, students, neighbors, and a host of other folks. I have no children, and I can't imagine the pain it must be to lose a child. But here's my two cents.

I wish I could say you get used to people dying. I never did. I don't want to. It tears a hole through me whenever somebody I love dies, no matter the circumstances. But I don't want it to "not matter". I don't want it to be something that just passes. My scars are a testament to the love and the relationship that I had for and with that person. And if the scar is deep, so was the love. So be it. Scars are a testament to life. Scars are a testament that I can love deeply and live deeply and be cut, or even gouged, and that I can heal and continue to live and continue to love. And the scar tissue is stronger than the original flesh ever was. Scars are a testament to life. Scars are only ugly to people who can't see.

As for grief, you'll find it comes in waves. When the ship is first wrecked, you're drowning, with wreckage all around. Everything floating around you reminds you of the beauty and magnificence of the ship that was, and is no more. And all you can do is float. You find some piece of the wreckage and you hang on for a while. Maybe it's some physical thing. Maybe a happy memory or a photograph; or a person who is also floating. For a while, all you can do is float. Stay alive.

In the beginning, the waves are 100 feet tall and crash over you without mercy. They come 10 seconds apart and don't give you time to catch your breath. All you can do is hang on and float. After a while, maybe weeks, maybe months, the waves are still 100 feet tall, but come further apart. When they come, they still crash all over you and wipe you out. But between, you can

'It's so curious: one can resist tears and 'behave' very well in the hardest hours of grief. But then someone makes you a friendly sign behind the window, or one notices that a flower that was in bud only yesterday has suddenly blossomed, or a letter slips from a drawer ... and everything collapses.'

COLETTE

breathe, you can function. You never know what's going to trigger the grief. It might be a song, a picture, a street intersection, the smell of a cup of coffee. It could be anything... and the wave comes crashing. But between waves, there is life.

Somewhere down the line, and it's different for everybody, you find that the waves are only 80 feet tall. Or 50 feet tall. And while they still come, they come further apart. You can see them coming. An anniversary, a birthday, or Christmas, or landing at O'Hare. You can see it coming, for the most part, and prepare yourself. And when it washes over you, you know that somehow you will, again, come out the other side. Soaking wet, sputtering, still hanging on to some tiny piece of the wreckage, but you'll come out. Take it from an old guy. The waves never stop coming, and somehow you don't really want them to. But you learn that you'll survive them. And other waves will come. And you'll survive them too. If you're lucky, you'll have lots of scars from lots of loves. And lots of shipwrecks.'

---

*

'You cannot stare straight into the face
of the sun, or death.'

FRANÇOIS DE LA ROCHEFOUCAULD

Many people who have lost someone find comfort in the book *Healing After Loss: Daily meditations for working through grief* by Martha Whitmore Hickman. Another beautiful book is *Our Souls at Night* by Kent Haruf, about two ageing people addressing loneliness after their spouses' deaths. It is incredibly moving and even more poignant when you learn that the author was dying as he wrote it.

Death and what it can teach us

In *Staring at the Sun* Irvin D. Yalom explores the subject of anxiety about death and how to lessen its impact. I cannot do the whole book justice here, but will outline some of the nuggets. He talks about 'awakening experiences', which could be as dramatic as a lucky escape from death, or as confrontational as being diagnosed with a life-threatening or life-ending disease, or more subtle everyday confrontations, such as a birthday with a '0' on the end, grief, divorce, children moving out or when a dream doesn't work out. These 'awakening experiences' are an abruption, but can have a positive transformative impact. Many medieval monks kept a skull in their cells to focus their minds on their mortality and therefore on how they

'The fear of death follows from the fear of life. A man
who lives fully is prepared to die at any time.'

AUTHOR UNKNOWN

should live their lives. Knowing that we are destined to die can motivate us to focus more on our everyday life. Saint Augustine said, 'It is only in the face of death that a man's self is born'.

I remember reading that you die twice. Once when you die and once when you are forgotten. Yalom describes 'rippling' as a way to ensure this doesn't happen: 'Rippling refers to the fact that each of us creates – often without our conscious intent or knowledge – concentric circles of influence that may affect others for years, even for generations.' It's not necessarily about our name or anything physical. We learned that lesson from Shelley's beautiful poem *Ozymandias* about an immense statue of the 'King of Kings' that now lies broken and abandoned in a wasteland: 'Look on my Works, ye Mighty, and despair!'

It can be small. It could be the impact you have on someone. 'Look for her among your friends' was the advice given to a daughter whose mother had died. Have a think about what ripples you might have created or will create. What would you like your legacy to be?

As well as taking comfort from the 'rippling' effect of good deeds, other advice from Yalom includes spending our lives doing what we

'The day which we fear is our last is
but the birthday of eternity.'

SENECA

love, so that we will not look back with regret, reaching out to form meaningful interpersonal relationships, and being bold in making necessary lifestyle changes that can bring us greater contentment. Live in the moment, he urges, and make each day count. This seems like obvious advice, but like the dieting and the meditation, it only works when you actually do it.

Yalom also advises us to 'keep in mind the advantage of remaining aware of death, of hugging its shadow to you. Such awareness can integrate the darkness with your spark of life and enhance your life while you still have it.'

It may be time I tackled the novel *The Death of Ivan Ilyich* by Leo Tolstoy, about a man who is about to die and realises he has not fully lived. Some books come into our lives at certain times for a reason and I hear this book knocking at my door.

Life after death

I heard the sublime singer Deva Premal (her album of mantras, 'The Essence', is one of my absolute favourites) and her unlikely partner, the grizzled cockney Miten, calmly talking about a dying person 'leaving their body'. No fear, just moving on to the next stage. That was an 'I'll have what she's having' moment for me. I need to learn more about it; I am at the base camp of Everest on this subject, but I don't want this life to be the end. I want to believe that there is something more and that one day I'll be reunited with my loved ones. If you don't feel the same and believe that when you die it's all over, that's fine too. With no partner to bounce these important issues off, it is important we ponder them alone, so that we prepare ourselves mentally for reaching that stage of our lives.

Death - the practicalities

Burial or cremation? Church or under a tree? Religious or humanist? Adele's 'When We Were Young?', Robbie Williams' 'Angels' or – God forbid – 'Wind Beneath My Wings'? Boring wooden box or a fab personalised coffin? (Go immediately to lifeart.com.au to see the possibilities!) Melancholy wake, or champagne party before you go? Friends as pallbearers? Ashes scattered or buried next to the family? And what would you like on your headstone?

These questions could be the basis for a fun party game were they not so important. And your relatives or friends will be so relieved if you have answered them in advance. It's to get the send-off that you want. The way you lived. So write it down and make sure someone knows where it is.

---

*
'As a well spent day brings happy sleep,
so a life well used brings happy death.'

LEONARDO DA VINCI

TAKE AWAYS

Spirituality gives you an internal reservoir of
courage and wisdom. It feeds your energy and
the way you project yourself to the world.

Learn to appreciate the benefits
of solitude and silence.

Listen to your intuition.

Identify your spiritual 'fastpass' from
walking a labyrinth, nature, a mantra, or
finding a patron saint or goddess.

Find a way into meditation that suits you.

Define your own spiritual 'necklace'
and the beads that go on it.

Give yourself the time to relax and maintain
equilibrium and then watch
synchronicity happen.

Think about the waves of grief and the
scars of love and your shipwrecks.

Reduce the fear of death so that it scares you
less and inspires you more.

Chapter 10

TAKING ACTION

How to get stuff done ∗ *Time* ∗ *Action boards*
∗ *Notebooks* ∗ *Accountability*

The world belongs to those who *do*. I hope this book encourages and inspires you to live the life you love, alone. I hope it has sown seeds. But there is no point in having thoughts, plans and dreams unless you splice them into your life. Don't live with a pile of shoulda, coulda, woulda... 'if only I had the time'. You have more time than you think. We spend on average over 46 days a year on the internet and 41 days watching TV (as opposed to 4.4 days reading). The tools we are given to work with are thoughts, words and actions, but the first two are redundant without the third. *Action* – any action – will lift a burden from your shoulders and propel you swiftly forwards. Ban the words 'I don't have time' and replace them with 'I will find the time'. Following are some suggestions to help you push off the diving board.

Be a postage stamp

Stick to one thing until you get there. If you spread yourself too widely, you risk spreading yourself too thinly. It's better to take aim at one thing and get it done; multi-tasking is a lie. Willpower is readily available but it is a finite resource, so use it early and wisely and it will serve you. These are some of the key principles of *The One Thing* by Gary Keller and Jay Papasan, who believe that extraordinary results are determined by how narrowly you focus. Think of the one thing you can do that will make an appreciable difference in each of the key areas of your life – living alone happily, relationships, health, finances, spirituality and so on.

Chunks of time

'Chunking down' is a business term used to describe the process of moving from broad, abstract ideas to smaller, more specific and manageable chunks. Activity is not the same as productivity and chunking down time is a good way of not letting it slip through your fingers. I don't want to be that annoying person who says 'Where has the time gone?' and at least if I have assigned my time, I'm one step ahead. When you take control of your time, you take control of your life.

The process of dividing up time comes with a pedigree. It is an ancient practice, well documented in Sara Maitland's *Book of Silence*. She talks about how people over the centuries lived in silence and how they navigated it. 'Drawing up "rules of life" – schedules or timetables and then exercising one's will to *stick to them* seems to be a necessary defence against the sluggish torpor of accidie and its attendant dangers.' ('Accidie' means listlessness or apathy.)

Whether I am at home or at work I split the day into hours like a timetable. It makes me more efficient and helps me squeeze the juice out of every day. So I can spend two hours writing, an hour going for a walk or to the gym, an hour doing emails, an hour clearing the decks and so on. You will know if you concentrate better in the evening or the morning ('owl' or 'fowl') and can schedule tasks accordingly. I am lucky in that time always flies for me and I always have things to do. If you don't and time is a burden, split your day into blocks and assign each one a purpose. For some people, shorter time spans work better. Author Francesco Cirillo swears by 25-minute *pomodoros* of concentrated effort, interspersed with short breaks ('the Pomodoro Technique' is named after the tomato-shaped kitchen timer he uses).

Small steps count

I keep reminding myself of this to make challenges less daunting. Taking the first steps along a path brings contentment and hope. It's interesting how action begets action and you quickly gain momentum.

Every day They say the way you spend your days is the way you spend your life, so make sure they count. Each day I complete between *one and three things.* That's not to say I don't get a lot more done in a day (I do), but this isn't just about finishing a work project or the ironing, it's about doing just one thing that notches me towards achieving my bigger goals. (Some people call these MITs or Most Important Tasks.) I try to do them as early in the day as possible, when my willpower is on full charge. A good litmus test of how well I'm doing is to ask myself, 'Did today matter?'

Every week I set myself between one and three small goals weekly and these tend to be quite specific. It could be walking at least 10,000 steps every day, finishing my tax return and sending 10 emails to friends. I write these goals on Post-it notes stuck in the kitchen and bathroom. (This is one of the joys of living alone – you can bare your Post-it note soul in private.)

An alternative is to focus on a theme a week for several weeks. It could be health, relationships, finances, work, home or spirituality. Alternatively, in her book *5:2 Your Life*, Kate Harrison offers a six-week plan with each week dedicated to one of the following: Discover, Connect, Simplify, Move, Relax and Do.

Every month At the beginning of the month I assign myself either a theme or a deadline for one thing I want to finish: writing this book, clearing the house of clutter, finalising a work project, or connecting with old friends.

Every year Every year I set myself just one big achievement. There are two ways to approach this One Major Thing. Either challenge yourself to learn a new skill – it could be a new language, or a new sport or hobby (look up classes right now!) – or finally, truthfully, nail some goals that have been kicking around for a while, like losing a specific amount of weight, working to make your home exactly the way you want it, organising your finances and saving up a certain amount of money, or getting certain relationships back on track. This doesn't have to be a January 1st thing. A new year starts on any day of the next 365 days. Mondays can be powerful enough. Just make sure that you can look at yourself in the mirror on day 365 and say, 'Nailed it'.

Breathing space

Our lives are full but little jolts of happiness can happen in the breathing spaces between the main events, if we are open to that. The sun shining on your face, a bird flying across the sky that only you can see, the touch of a friend's hand on your shoulder, an unexpected uplifting email from a friend. As children we played at avoiding the cracks in the pavement because the bears might get us. Now I think the cracks are where the real beauty lies. Bring on the bears!

What would Oprah do?

If you are feeling lethargic, out of sorts or unmotivated, slip into someone else's skin. How would the best you, your alter ego and/or someone you respect approach this situation? Or pretend you're being filmed for your own reality show. How do you want to be perceived? I find this quick mind-shift a great catalyst.

Curate an action board

I don't believe you make a vision board and, wallop, it manifests. However, I do enjoy both the process and the end result of making my ambitions visually concrete. More action board than vision board. My board captures the joys of living alone and the plans and dreams I have. It makes me feel good as soon as I look at it. Throughout this book, you might have liked some ideas and rejected others, like a hen pecking at grain, instinctively picking and choosing what will work best for you and your 'self-keeping' plan for the future. Capture some of them on your board.

Pick images and ephemera carefully, with the eyes of a curator. The word 'curate' comes from the Latin *cura* or 'care', meaning to carefully select and edit the items you want and place them together to give them greater meaning. Every image has to earn its keep. 'Curation' is a word very much in vogue (and overused in the context of the internet) and is traditionally used in connection with museums and art galleries, with the curator choosing which works are selected and how they are displayed. It is a rare talent that your gut recognises when it is done truly well – the best and wittiest example of curation I have ever seen is at the Hunting Museum in Paris (Musée de la Chasse et de la Nature).

You can use Pinterest to make a virtual pinboard, although I prefer a physical board, but either way you can display the finished version as wallpaper on your computer screen or phone. I have experimented with different methods of making boards and think I've finally nailed it. Buy a sheet of 90 x 60 cm foamcore board at an office supply shop, cutting it smaller if you prefer. I like to cover mine with fabric, so I use the board that has an adhesive side. Simply stick your fabric on, buy some long pins and you're good to go. Foamcore is very light, so it is easy to pin and re-pin images – nothing is stuck down permanently, which is how it should be, as your board will change.

Look online and in magazines (and in this book!) for quotations and images that resonate and inspire, and look in junk and antique shops for ephemera and other bits and bobs. I scour the internet to buy things with the number '1' on them – old tin numbers from petrol stations, a 1 from a cricket scoreboard and an old price tag. I am a 1! I have also taken photographs of moments that epitomise my solo life: watching the dawn sky from my bedroom window; sitting by my little fire pit with a glass of wine and roasting marshmallows in winter; my newly made crispy white bed. All are solitary pleasures, capturing a solo life well led, along with my plans for the future. You can add tickets, postcards and trinkets ('tchotchkes', as my American Jewish friend would call them) to bring it to life. There are no rules – it is just for you. Sometimes I make smaller boards if I want to address a specific issue in more detail.

It is also interesting to reflect on the board after time has passed: what has changed, what still works and what is no longer relevant? You instinctively make course corrections, just like moving the steering wheel slightly when you are driving along a straight road. It is a nudge in the direction of action.

The notebook system

I find it helpful to have several notebooks on the go. You probably have a system that works best for you – this is mine. I have an A4 hardcover journal (a lovely, ribbon-tied, marbled paper-covered book that I bought in Italy), for my eyes only. Do you remember at school when we used scrap paper for 'workings out'? My journal is where I do my own personal 'workings out'. I write how I feel, motivate myself and collect inspirational ideas I have heard or seen. It helps shape me and is where I talk things through with myself. However, I feel under no obligation to write something every day.

———————————— ✳ ————————————

'You must live in the present, launch yourself on every wave, find your eternity in each moment. Fools stand on their island opportunities and look toward another land. There is no other land; there is no other life but this.'

HENRY DAVID THOREAU

I use four other books too:

- A spiral-bound counter book – long and thin for my ongoing 'to do list', with pages dedicated to work, writing, the house and so on.
- An A5 Moleskin notebook in my handbag with a pen stuffed in the spine for writing down recommendations, things I see, or even phrases I hear on the radio. Each one fills up in about a month. Then I go through them and copy down the 'keepers' into another book.
- A tiny spiral-bound pad for shopping lists etc.
- A Post-it notepad for my three-point 'Do Today' prompt.

I prefer physical notebooks, but digitally minded mates swear by Evernote, which is a cross-platform app that serves many purposes – as a journal, a note-taking tool, digital filing cabinet, recipe-keeper and many more.

Develop rituals

Aristotle said, 'We are what we repeatedly do,' so it makes sense to do those things we 'repeatedly do' *well*. And that's where rituals come in.

Since I have lived alone, I have unconsciously established routines and rituals. I like the rhythm, pulse and punctuation they give my life. What's the difference between a ritual and a routine? Good question, young Grasshopper. Both are repeated actions, but a ritual is done with purpose and intent, with a bit of reverence and ceremony thrown in. A ritual is deliberate, whereas a routine is unthinking. A ritual can become a routine, but rarely the other way round. Still with me?

'Ritual and routine ... seem to be two sides of the same coin – while routine aims to make the chaos of every day life more containable and controllable, ritual aims to imbue the mundane with an element of the magical.' Maria Popova at BrainPickings.org

The easiest way to introduce simple rituals into your life is to develop a morning routine that helps set the framework for the day. Here are a few ideas:

- The first things you see and do each morning are important. My bedside table always has fresh flowers and a photograph of my children. My action board is on my desk and in full sight. Before I put my feet down, I think about what sort of a day I'm going to have and capture it in one positive adjective.
- Open the curtains as soon as you wake up and have a beautiful glass of water with lemon juice by your bed to sip first thing. If you've had a strong dream, quickly write it down. Meditate for 10 minutes, maybe striking a Tibetan singing bowl to get you started.
- Many people enjoy Qi Gong exercises after waking to give a boost of energy. Try the 10-minute 'Morning Qi Ritual by Lee Holden' on YouTube. Or just stretch.
- I set out my go-to weekday breakfast (berries, yoghurt and oats) in the fridge the night before.

'Every day a thread makes a skein in the year.'

DUTCH PROVERB

- I do 20 quick things to get the house ready for the day – emptying the dishwasher, sorting laundry, putting papers away, taking out the rubbish, feeding the dog etc. I am clearing the decks before the start of a performance, priming my day.
- Some people like affirmations, some don't. If you do, find a book of daily affirmations that suits you. Try *Inneractions: Visions to Bring Your Inner and Outer World into Harmony* by Stephen C. Paul and Gary Max Collins. Or just pick an oracle card (see Chapter 9).
- Other people swear by writing Morning Pages (another idea from *The Artist's Way* by Julia Cameron), which are three pages of longhand stream of consciousness, chronicling anything that comes into your mind. Julia Cameron describes them as 'using a dustbuster on your mind'. This is a clearing exercise – if you get all your negative stuff down on paper, it doesn't then interfere with your day and makes room for more profound thoughts.
- Landmines that sabotage my morning ritual are: drinking too much the night before, sleeping in, eating a big breakfast, looking at emails or social media first thing or watching breakfast TV, so I never, ever do them.

'Productivity is about doing things you've never been able to do before.'

FRANZ KAFKA

Another lovely ritual I have started to embrace at the other end of the day is the 15-minute Violet Hour. This marks the end of the working day and the beginning of the evening at about six o'clock and is a time to lower emotional and mental defences and relax.

Bernard DeVoto coined the phrase in *The Hour*: 'This is the violet hour, the hour of hush and wonder, when the affections glow and valour is reborn, when the shadows deepen along the edge of the forest and we believe that, if we watch carefully, at any moment we may see the unicorn.'

The Violet Hour doesn't have to involve alcohol, but it is nice to have a drink that involves some kind of mixing, to add another touch of ceremony. Put on some music – no phone, no computer – and slink into the evening. I find it a bit like a gentle evening meditation.

Rituals and routines have been useful to me and I am not alone:

'It's a simple act, but doing it the same way each [day] habitualises it – makes it repeatable, easy to do. It reduces the chance that I skip it or do it differently... when you [follow daily rituals], they impel you to get started. Whether it's the act of carrying a hot coffee mug to an outdoor porch, or the rock'n'roll that gets a painter revved up to splash color on a canvas, or the stillness of a herb garden that puts a chef in a culinary trance, moving inside each of these routines gives you no choice but to do something. It's Pavlovian: follow the routine, get a creative payoff.' Twyla Tharp, *The Creative Habit: Learn It and Use It for Life*

Habits are Ritual's responsible but slightly boring older sister. To live a successful life alone, you have to have discipline. Being disciplined doesn't come easily to me, but when you re-interpret it as simply acting out good habits repeatedly, it seems less daunting and more attainable.

Keep yourself accountable

You are responsible for keeping your life on track. Accountable people don't give up. When they face bumps in the road, they find a way around them. Sometimes it's useful to have a reminder of how strong you are. I find wearing a piece of jewellery with my name on it helps me remember. It is hard to articulate, but since I have lived alone, my first name seems to have acquired a greater significance. It's all I have. It's me in a word: my calling card and my essence. It epitomises my independence. I have a silver 'Jane' dog tag and I wear it every day.

Search 'name jewellery' online – a good place to start is etsy.com. You will know what suits you best: a necklace, bracelet or a ring. You may want to add some other words or a saying that is important to you. If you don't want to buy more jewellery, think about having an existing ring engraved with your name.

Be bold. Be big

We weren't put on the planet to be small. Carve your own path and think big. Don't order from the set menu. Set your pitch to a higher frequency; run a few volts through it; put running spikes on it. Challenge yourself and be ambitious in your dreams.

SOME FINAL TAKE AWAYS

Chinese philosopher Lao Tzu said,
'Contentment is the greatest treasure',
meaning the way to find happiness is just
to *want what you already have*. Sometimes
I catch myself spending so much time
planning an upcoming trip (the map, the
walks, the menus of the restaurant, the
opening times of the museums and so on)
that my day-to-day life takes a
back seat. *Carpe diem.*

We are responsible for changing
society's perception of people who
live alone. We need to be walking
advertisements for our tribe!

Every day is a new start. What you do
today is what matters most.

Enjoy your life living with yourself.
I believe in you. You've got this.

*I'd love to hear how your path unfolds, so do
reach out to me via theartoflivingalone.com.au*

Invictus by William Ernest Henley

The word *invictus* is Latin for 'unconquerable'. Henley's poem describes every person who has had struggles and come through them.

William Ernest Henley was an Englishman, who lost his bookseller father when he was just a teenager. At 12 he contracted tuberculosis and had one leg amputated below the knee; the other foot was saved through radical surgery. As he healed, he began to write poems, including *Invictus*. Its theme is the will to survive in the face of severe tests. The poem was recited by Nelson Mandela during his 27-year imprisonment – it gave him courage and strength to endure the time in his tiny cell.

The first verse acknowledges despair that manifests itself as darkness. Henley isn't asking for help but thanks (as an agnostic would) 'whatever gods there may be' for the immense strength already within himself. In the second verse he is still standing tall, never complaining, despite the blows coming his way. He'd rather take a beating than give in; he is brave and looks his problems straight in the eye. The third verse indicates worse may lie in the years ahead – including death (literally or metaphorically). However, his inner strength has prepared him for this and he is not afraid – not now, or in the future.

The final verse refers to Judgement Day, when our bad deeds will be added up and written on a scroll. Henley recognises that even then he alone is responsible for his soul, his fate. His resilience and self-possession give him complete control over his destiny.

Remember: you alone choose your path.

Invictus

Out of the night that covers me,
Black as the Pit from pole to pole,
I thank whatever gods may be
For my unconquerable soul.

In the fell clutch of circumstance
I have not winced nor cried aloud.
Under the bludgeonings of chance
My head is bloody, but unbowed.

Beyond this place of wrath and tears
Looms but the Horror of the shade,
And yet the menace of the years
Finds, and shall find, me unafraid.

It matters not how strait the gate,
How charged with punishments the scroll,
I am the master of my fate:
I am the captain of my soul.

Coda

Full disclosure – life never goes according to plan. As I finish writing this book my university-aged daughter is moving back in with me and I no longer live alone, at least for the time being. Much as I love every hair on her out-till-four-in-the-morning-head, I realise how happy I was living alone. I taught myself how to do it well and I miss it... Watch this space.

FURTHER READING

Abey, A & A Ford, *How Much is Enough?*, A&B Publishers, Sydney, 2007.

Anderson, C M & S Stewart, *Flying Solo: single women in midlife*, W.W. Norton, New York, 1995.

Anderson, J, *A Weekend to Change Your Life*, Broadway Books, New York, 2006.

Anderson, J, *A Year by the Sea: thoughts of an unfinished woman*, Broadway Books, New York, 1999.

Baker, J, *A Man is Not a Financial Plan: investing for wealth and independence*, Allen & Unwin, Sydney, 2007.

Buchan, M, *Over it: How to live above your circumstances and beyond yourself*, SPARK Publications, Charlotte, 2013.

Buettner, D, *The Blue Zones: Lessons for living longer from the people who've lived longest*, National Geographic Society, Washington, 2010.

Cameron, J, *The Artist's Way*, Pan Macmillan, London, 2001.

The Complete Cooking for Two Cookbook, America's Test Kitchen, Boston, 2014.

Crowley, C & H S Lodge, *Younger Next Year for Women*, Workman, New York, 2005.

Deresiewicz, W, 'Solitude and Leadership', speech delivered October 2009, transcript available from TheAmericanScholar.org.

Falk, F, *On My Own: The art of being a woman alone*, Three Rivers Press, New York, 2007.

Feldon, B, *Living Alone and Loving It*, Fireside, New York, 2003.

Ferrari-Adlerby, J, *Alone in the Kitchen with an Eggplant: Confessions of cooking for one and dining alone*, Riverhead, New York, 2007.

Fisher, L, *Celebrating Time Alone: Stories of splendid solitude*, Beyond Words Publishing, Hillsboro, 2001.

Goldner, N, *Living Solo*, PhD published by the author, 2013

Harrison, K, *5:2 Your Life: Get healthy, happy and slim*, Orion, London, 2014.

Hartley, A, *Love the Life You Live: Ten steps for happier living, a life coaching process*, Hart Publishing, Mona Vale, 2000.

Harv Eker, T, *Secrets of the Millionaire Mind: Mastering the inner game of wealth*, Harper Collins, New York, 2005.

Johnson, F, 'Going it Alone' in *Harper's Magazine*, April 2015

Keller, G & J Papasan, *The ONE Thing: The Surprisingly Simple Truth Behind Extraordinary Results*, Bard Press, 2013. www.the1thing.com

Klinenberg, E, *Going Solo: The extraordinary rise and surprising appeal of living alone*, Penguin, New York, 2012.

Lawson, N, *How to Eat*, Random House, New York, 1998.

Lesser, E, *The Seeker's Guide*, Villard Books, New York, 1999.

Maitland, S, *A Book of Silence*, Granta Books, London, 2009.

Morrow Lindbergh, A, *Gift from the Sea*, Pantheon Books, New York, 2005.

Orman, S, *Women and Money: Owning the power to control your destiny*, Spiegel & Grau, New York, 2007.

Pape, S, *The Barefoot Investor: Five steps to financial freedom*, Pluto Press, Melbourne, 2007.

Robinson, K, *Finding Your Element: How to discover your talents and passions and transform your life*, Penguin, New York, 2014.

Rufus, A, *Party of One: The loners' manifesto*, Avalon Travel Publishing, Chicago, 2003.

Schacter-Shalomi, Z, *From Age-ing to Sage-ing*, Little, Brown & Company, New York, 2014.

Rufus, A, *Unworthy: How to stop hating yourself*, TarcherPerigee, New York, 2015.

Shulman, A K, *Drinking the Rain*, North Point Press, New York, 1995.

Smith, D, *One is Fun!* Coronet Books, London, 1987.

Solomon, A, *The Noonday Demon: An anatomy of depression*, Vintage, London, 2016.

Waugh, J, *The Solo Traveler's Handbook*, Full Flight Press, Toronto, 2011.

Whitmore Hickhan, M, *Healing After Loss: Daily meditations for working through grief*, Harper Collins, New York, 1994.

Yalom, I D, *Staring at the Sun. Overcoming the terror of death*, Jossey Bass, Hoboken, 2009.

Yonan, J, *Serve Yourself: Nightly adventures in cooking for one*, Ten Speed Press, New York, 2011.

INDEX

Acknowledgements

Thanks to my agent, Fiona Inglis from Curtis Brown,
who has always had confidence in this book. Also a huge
thanks to everyone at Murdoch Books for helping shepherd
my words into the world, especially Corinne Roberts,
Jane Price, Julie Mazur Tribe, Madeleine Kane, Fleur Anson,
Lou Playfair and Carol Warwick.

Also thanks to my children, Alex and Kate, and all the
wonderful soloists I have met while researching this book.
We are a special tribe.

Jane Mathews has had plenty of practice living alone,
having travelled all over the world during her successful
career in advertising. She has previously written passionately
about middle age in *Midlife Manifesto*. Finding herself living
alone, post-unanticipated divorce, in *The Art of Living Alone
and Loving It* Jane candidly shares her tips for navigating the
sometimes treacherous shallows of solo life. She explains
what has helped her create a life rich in possibilities,
in friendships, in challenges, in personal rituals and in
scrumptious meals for one. (Vietnamese claypot chicken,
anyone?) She lives behind a red front door in Sydney with
Rory the Airedale terrier (who won't be troubling Mensa)
and piles of unfinished craft projects.